Learning from Errors at School and at Work

Research in Vocational Education

edited by
Eveline Wuttke • Jürgen Seifried

Volume 1

Editorial board
Editors in chief:
Eveline Wuttke, Goethe University Frankfurt, Germany
Jürgen Seifried, Konstanz University, Germany

Editorial board:
Josef Aff, Wirtschaftsuniversität Wien, Vienna, Austria
Stephen Billet, Griffith University, Brisbane, Australia
Thomas Deissinger, Konstanz University, Germany
Rolf Dubs, St. Gallen University, Switzerland
Erika Ekström, Ministry of Employment, Stockholm, Sweden
Richard Fortmüller, Wirtschaftsuniversität Wien, Vienna, Austria
Gerhard Minnameier, Goethe University Frankfurt, Germany
Ana Luisa de Oliveira Pires, Escola Superior de Educação, Instituto Politécnico de Setúbal, Portugal
Kestutis Pukelis, Vytautas Magnus University, Kaunas, Lithuania
Tomas Sabaliauskas, Vytautas Magnus University, Kaunas, Lithuania
Detlef Sembill, Bamberg University, Germany
Peter F.E. Sloane, Paderborn University, Germany

Eveline Wuttke
Jürgen Seifried (eds.)

Learning from Errors at School and at Work

Verlag Barbara Budrich
Opladen • Berlin • Farmington Hills, MI 2012

Bibliografische Information der Deutschen Nationalbibliothek
Die Deutsche Nationalbibliothek verzeichnet diese Publikation in der Deutschen
Nationalbibliografie; detaillierte bibliografische Daten sind im Internet über
http://dnb.d-nb.de abrufbar.

Gedruckt auf säurefreiem und alterungsbeständigem Papier.

Alle Rechte vorbehalten.
© 2012 Verlag Barbara Budrich, Opladen, Berlin & Farmington Hills, MI
www.budrich-verlag.de

ISBN   978-3-86649-415-2

Das Werk einschließlich aller seiner Teile ist urheberrechtlich geschützt. Jede Verwertung außerhalb der engen Grenzen des Urheberrechtsgesetzes ist ohne Zustimmung des Verlages unzulässig und strafbar. Das gilt insbesondere für Vervielfältigungen, Übersetzungen, Mikroverfilmungen und die Einspeicherung und Verarbeitung in elektronischen Systemen.

Umschlaggestaltung: disegno visuelle kommunikation, Wuppertal – www.disenjo.de
Druck: paper & tinta, Warschau
Printed in Europe

Contents

Learning from Errors, Surprise or rather from Errorless Training? Reflections on Basic and Applied Research 9
Eveline Wuttke and Jürgen Seifried

1 What's Wrong With It? – Kinds and Inferential Mechanics of Errors and Mistakes 13
Gerhard Minnameier

1.1	Problems: How to Get Wrong Things Wrong 13
1.2	Inferences: How to Get It Right 15
1.3	Mistakes: How to Get It Wrong 20
1.4	Errors: How to be Right and Still Go Wrong 24
1.5	Instruction and Construction: How to Get It Right 25

2 Learning from Mistakes – till a Challenge for Research and Business Practice 31
Christian Harteis and Katrin Buschmeyer

2.1	Introduction 31
2.2	Mistakes and Business Organisation 32
2.3	Explanations 34
2.4	State of Educational Research 41
2.5	Challenges for Research and Business Practice 43
2.6	Conclusion 45

3 Learning from Errors – Strategies for Accounting Lessons – Outline of a Research Project 49

Maxi Link

3.1	The Need for a Cognitive Perspective on Learning from Errors	49
3.2	The Inferential Access: Identifying, Classifying and Dealing with Errors	50
3.3	Methodological Approach: The Instructional Support and Analysis of Learning from Errors	55
3.4	Prospects to Realizing the Research Project	61

4 The Student Perspective on Dealing with Errors in Mathematics Class 65

Aiso Heinze, Stefan Ufer, Stefanie Rach and Kristina Reiss

4.1	Introduction	65
4.2	Theoretical Background	65
4.3	Aims and Research Questions	68
4.4	Method	69
4.5	Results	71
4.6	Discussion	76

5 Negative Knowledge of Primary School Teachers – Results from an Explorative Study 81

Martin Gartmeier, Katharina Lorenzer, Hans Gruber and Helmut Heid

5.1	Introduction	81
5.2	Theoretical Background	82
5.3	Method	85
5.4	Results	86

5.5	Discussion	89
5.6	Conclusion	91

6 Teachers' Knowledge about Domain Specific Student Errors ... 95

Janosch M. Türling, Jürgen Seifried and Eveline Wuttke

6.1	Professional Error Competence (PEC)	95
6.2	Student Errors in the Domain of Bookkeeping	97
6.3	Method	99
6.4	Findings	102
6.5	Conclusion	106

7 Errors, Emotions, and Learning in the Workplace – Findings from a Diary Study within VET ... 111

Andreas Rausch

7.1	Learning from Errors in the Workplace	111
7.2	Data and Method	114
7.3	Results	119
7.4	Discussion	122

8 Professional Handling of Errors in the Workplace 127

Alexander Baumgartner and Jürgen Seifried

8.1	Introduction	127
8.2	Professional Competence of Company Trainers	128
8.3	Concept of an Empirical Study for Measuring Company Trainers' Error Competence	131
8.4	Summary and Outlook	138

9 Learning From Errors – Perspectives from Basic Research 143

Andy J. Wills

9.1	Introduction	143
9.2	The Importance of Errors	143
9.3	The Importance of Elaborated Feedback	146
9.4	The Importance of Extended Practice	149
9.5	Conclusion	151

Learning from Errors, Surprise or rather from Errorless Training? Reflections on Basic and Applied Research

It is commonly held that it is possible to develop professional competence by learning from errors at school and in the workplace. Several disciplines study how teachers should best react to students' errors; namely, Pedagogy, Psychology, Medical Science, Neurology and Engineering Sciences (e.g. Bauer 2008; Graber 2009; Mehl/Wehner 2008; Oser/Spychiger 2005; Weingardt 2004). Consequently, in the field of teaching-learning-research, increasing effort has been directed towards identifying error types and the possibility of learning from errors as well as analysing how teachers' behaviour influences students' chances of learning from errors (e.g. Baumert et al. 2010; Heinze 2004; Seidel/Prenzel 2007). In this context, a key aspect of learning from errors is an 'error-friendly' learning environment with elaborate feedback from the teacher which supports learning from errors. However, evidence from lab-based research suggests that, rather than errors, it is the element of surprise that drives error based learning, and moreover, the elaboration of an error can lead to perseveration. And some results indicate that it is not a question of how elaborate feedback is, but how well it fits the learning mode (c.f. Wills in this volume). This volume presents texts from lab-based and applied research that investigate the subject of how and under what conditions learning from errors can occur.

Beginning with a more theoretical approach, the general theory of inferential reasoning, Minnameier addresses questions of how learners get things wrong, what types of mistakes are made and how instruction and construction can help learners to get it right. This is followed by Harteis and Buschmeyer's reflection on how learning from mistakes is still a challenge for research and business practice. In addition to reporting typical mistakes in business practice and providing plausible explanations, they show that although various theoretical and empirical approaches have been developed within educational research to understand learning from errors, numerous challenges for research and business practice remain.

The subsequent texts move from theoretical considerations to applied research: One introduces the outline of a research project, while others present results from various studies. In her project, Link returns to Minnameier's inferential theory to outline a microgenetic study designed to analyze learning from errors and develop instructional support following errors.

The following texts present results regarding learning from errors and the methods teachers and trainers utilize to deal with errors. Starting with a study situated in the context of mathematics learning, Heinze, Ufer, Rach and Reiss focus on the error-handling activities that teachers and students perform in mathematics lessons. Their main questions are how students experience the actions of their teachers in error situations and how students use their own errors as learning opportunities. Results show that teachers consider errors to be a natural part of the learning process, but that they do not have well established instructional strategies on how to actually use errors productively and how to teach their students to use errors as learning opportunities.

Gartmeier, Lorenzer, Gruber and Heid direct their focus towards teachers' learning processes. They show how teachers' and trainee teachers' negative knowledge (knowledge on how things are not and which strategies do not work) is developed by way of making mistakes and how this helps them act in critical classroom situations.

The next study is situated in the context of vocational schools. It analyses teachers' knowledge about domain specific errors. Türling, Seifried and Wuttke argue that a teacher's ability to diagnose student errors and use them constructively in the classroom is a key aspect of teacher professionalism. They are able to demonstrate that the ability to identify and to correct errors is rather low, especially with students in teacher education programs and teachers who are still in practical training. Contrary to this, most participants perceive their own competence as being rather high. Again, it is especially students and pre-service teachers who tend to overestimate their ability.

Rausch focuses on the relationship between errors, learning from errors, and emotions linked to errors in the workplace. He uses questionnaires and internet-based work diaries to record work tasks, perceived learning and emotional experience to show that errors generally occur when tackling new and difficult tasks or communicating with externals. Initially, errors at the workplace are connected with negative emotions, but this association changes over time.

The study by Baumgartner and Seifried is also situated in the context of workplace learning. The authors outline the conception of a study focusing on trainer competence in supporting learning from errors in work situations. Empirical findings on typical errors made by apprentices are used to construct picture vignettes employed as prompts for the analysis of pedagogical action in error situations.

If we take a closer look at the studies that are presented in this volume, it becomes quite apparent that errors and the handling of errors are seen as an important aspect of learning in both schools and the workplace. If, as previously suggested, a key aspect of this context is an 'error-friendly' learning environment and elaborate feedback from the teacher, then the results obtained in applied research thus far suggest that there is a good possibility that learning from errors can occur. At the very least, it can be shown that few learning environments sanction errors or are error adverse (Heinze et al. in this volume). However, the feedback component presents a very different situation: teachers do not have well established strategies on how to use errors (Heinze et al.). This leads us to the conclusion that learning from errors can only partly occur. The situation becomes even more complicated when we take into account the results of basic research which suggest that the element of surprise is more conducive to learning. Perhaps then, learning from errors is not a question of well-elaborated feedback but of feedback that fits with the learning mode (Wills in this volume). Only one thing is certain: much research is still needed if we are to answer the question as to how and under what conditions people learn from errors.

Frankfurt and Konstanz
July 2011

Eveline Wuttke and Jürgen Seifried

References

Bauer, J. (2008): Fehler und Lernen aus Fehlern – Die Notwendigkeit deskriptiver und kumulativer empirischer Forschung. In: *Erwägen, Wissen, Ethik*, 19, pp. 306-310.
Baumert, J./Kunter, M./Blum, W./Brunner, M./Voss, T./ Jordan, A./Klusmann, U./Krauss, S./Neubrand, M./Yi-Miau, T. (2010): Teachers' mathematical knowledge, cognitive activation in the classroom, and student progress. In: *American Educational Research Journal*, 47 (1), pp. 133-180.
Graber, M L. (2009): Educational strategies to reduce diagnostic error: can you teach this stuff? In: *Advances in Health Science Education*, 14, pp. 63-69.
Heinze, A. (2004): Zum Umgang mit Fehlern im Unterrichtsgespräch der Sekundarstufe I. Theoretische Grundlegung, Methode und Ergebnisse einer Videostudie. In: *Journal für Mathematik-Didaktik*, 25, pp. 221-245.
Mehl, K./Wehner, T. (2008): Über die Schwierigkeiten, aus Fehlern zu lernen. Auf der Suche nach einer angemessenen methodischen Vorgehensweise zur Untersuchung von Handlungsfehlern. In: *Erwägen, Wissen, Ethik*, 19, pp. 265-273.
Oser, F./Spychiger, M. (2005): *Lernen ist schmerzhaft. Zur Theorie des negativen Wissens und zur Praxis der Fehlerkultur*. Weinheim/Basel: Beltz.
Seidel, T./Prenzel, M. (2007): Wie Lehrpersonen Unterricht wahrnehmen und einschätzen – Erfassung pädagogisch-psychologischer Kompetenzen mit Videosequenzen. In: *Zeitschrift für Erziehungswissenschaft*, Sonderheft 8, pp. 201-216.
Weingardt, M. (2004): *Fehler zeichnen uns aus. Transdisziplinäre Grundlagen zur Theorie und Produktivität des Fehlers in Schule und Arbeitswelt*. Bad Heilbrunn: Klinkhardt.

1 What's Wrong With It? – Kinds and Inferential Mechanics of Errors and Mistakes

Gerhard Minnameier

1.1 Problems: How to Get Wrong Things Wrong

Winston Churchill is supposed to have said that all men make mistakes, but that only wise men learn from their mistakes. Given that learning from mistakes is not only a bare necessity, but is also hailed in today's educational theory (c.f. e.g. Lundquist 1999; Weingardt 2004; Cannon/Edmondson 2005; Oser/Spychiger 2005; Meyer/Seidel/Prenzel 2006; Yerushalmi/Polingher 2006; Gartmeier/Bauer/Gruber/Heid 2008; Harteis/Bauer/Gruber 2008; Seifried/Wuttke 2010), and assuming that a good deal of learners – men and women – are not (yet) wise, the key question would be: How we can get the less wise learners to learn from their mistakes?

A key problem which prevents learners from learning from their mistakes is certainly that they do not know what is wrong or what they have done wrong. What's more, teachers have to see where and how their students fail in order to be able to help them along. Therefore, inasmuch as teachers and learners fail to understand mistakes in the first place, learning from them can scarcely occur. Hence, there is a need to know what is wrong when students go wrong.

Mistakes and errors can be manifold.[1] Some fail to properly represent the task or situation they are in. Others choose the wrong approach or strategy, draw false conclusions or follow a certain route although they could know that it is futile. These are just a few possibilities which make clear how important it is to know, where or in what respect someone goes wrong.

However, existing classifications do not seem to yield us a systematic and pedagogically useful picture of the various kinds of mistakes, at least inasmuch as they relate to reasoning. In this respect they are either too superficial, because they relate more to action schemes and effects rather than the underlying reasoning processes, or they mix cognitive stages and processes and thus confound important aspects of cognitive (dis)function that ought to be kept separate (as will be shown later in the paper).

---

[1] As will be explained in more detail below, we differentiate between errors and mistakes as two distinct kinds of failures. However, "error" is sometimes also used as a general term that encompasses different kinds of failures (see e. g. Reason 1990).

As regards the first point, Dörner and Schaub (1994) for example distinguish types of errors according to phases of action regulation. These phases are labelled "goal-elaboration", "hypothesis-formation", "forecasting", "planning", "monitoring", and "self-reflection". Of course, this may be regarded as an ideal sequence of sub-processes in conscious and rational agency. However, goal-elaboration already requires profound understanding of the given situation and its affordances. Hence, some kind of "hypothesis" concerning the relevant system must be at hand. "Hypothesis formation" as such is then linked with "information collection" (ibid., p. 439), which are clearly separate processes (for one must first collect information in order to derive hypotheses on this informational ground). What's more, goal elaboration equally requires the collection of information in the first place. The next step, "prognoses" can be regarded as consequences to be drawn from hypotheses. However, Dörner and Schaub discuss the problem that "(w)e have difficulties in understanding the characteristics of developments simply because we forget so much, and so the images we form about developments are often too simple" (ibid., p. 441). Does this not mean that the hypotheses that we have set up in the first place are inappropriate? And with respect to planning processes, Dörner and Schaub hold that "(w)ith complex systems the main mistake of planning seems to be to disregard side- and long-term effects, which nearly every action will have" (ibid., p. 443). Is this not a problem of false or oversimplified prognoses which in turn depend on our hypotheses? Without discussing these matters and the other phases further, we can conclude that such a classification is not systematic enough and follows a logic of action rather than a logic of thought.

As to the point of confounding structures and processes, a good and well known example is Rasmussen's (1980) and Reason's (1987; 1990) differentiation of "skill-based", "rule-based", and "knowledge-based" mistakes:

At the skill-based level, the informational content is in the form of *signals*, and performance is governed by stored patterns of preprogrammed instructions (schemata) represented as analogue structures in a time-space domain. At the rule-based level, performance is guided by *signs* relating to stored rules or productions (of the IF <situation> THEN <action> form). The knowledge-based level comes into play in novel situations for which actions must be planned on-line, through the manipulation of *symbols*. The skill- and rule-based levels most involve the schematic control mode, while the attentional mode predominates at the skill-based level (Reason 1987: 64).

The main problem with this classification is that structures are confounded with processes of knowledge activation versus generation. The knowledge-based level obviously consists in the original and creative generation of new knowledge ("symbols"; although the differentiation between *signs* and *symbols* is not clear here). However, such processes can lead either to new rules or to higher order theories, which certainly creates an important distinction. What's more, the creation of new rules can be effected by simply contriving rules by trial and error or actually deriving them from some higher order understanding, which points to another important difference unaccounted for.

This difference is so important, because it is one thing – and an essential cognitive *process* – to create or to generate new knowledge items, even if they be only new rules or schemata. It is another question – one of structure – at which level of abstraction (in a broadly Piagetian sense) the reasoning takes place. The distinction of "skills", "rules" and "knowledge" obviously points to such levels of cognitive functioning.

What remains in the dark, however, is the specification of the different cognitive processes, into which mistakes might sneak. And this seems to be a general deficiency, above and beyond the work of J. Reason. The present paper will be devoted to revealing the cognitive processes which underlie both correct and incorrect reasoning, and to the explication of the respective types of mistakes.

In the following section a general theory of inferential reasoning which encompasses abduction, deduction, and induction will be presented. It is pointed out in Section 3 where mistakes can take place in these inferences. As all inferences can be subdivided into distinct steps, there are various possibilities for results to go wrong within each inferential type.

In Section 4 another form of failure, which we call error, will be discussed. The notion of "error" to be used in the present paper requires that the epistemic subject is unaware of their failure and is not in a cognitive position to see the mistake. This aspect of cognitive restrictedness points to the general problem of cognitive structures hinted at above. We will not be able to discuss this problem at sufficient depth in the present paper, but it will at least be put in context to some extent in Section 5, which focuses on an overall framework of learning and development from the processual and structural perspective. This yields a general understanding of how learners learn from their mistakes and how teachers can teach them this vital skill.

1.2   Inferences: How to Get It Right

We are only able to understand and analyse mistakes properly if we have an appropriate understanding of correct reasoning. Since this is the proper realm of logic, we should try to reconstruct the logic of thought in its various forms. Today, the notion of logic is often reduced to deductive logic, but as it is clear that there are also non-deductive inferences, it is perhaps wise to take a broader view on logic (see e.g. Copi/Cohen 2004: 4). Furthermore, we know that Popper's attempt to build the logic of scientific discovery solely on deductive inferences hast failed (see Gardner 2001; Minnameier 2004).

On top of this, if we accept that knowledge is constructed rather than simply picked up, and if the notion of knowledge requires certainty on the part of the epistemic subject, then new knowledge must be actually and literally inferred from prior knowledge plus experience based on that prior knowledge. However, this cannot be effected by means of deduction, because deductive inferences only yield necessary consequences that are already implicit in prior knowledge, but nothing beyond that.

An interesting approach to such a comprehensive logic of thought goes back to Charles Sanders Peirce, who also held that "logic is, in the main, criticism of reasoning as good or bad" (1902/1974: 76 [CP 2.144]). His theory comprises three inferential types: abduction, deduction, and induction.

Peirce's inferential triad is widely discussed today (see e.g. Gabbay/ Woods 2005; Magnani 2009; Minnameier 2004; 2010a, Campos 2011). However, there is still some confusion about the meaning of those three inferences, in particular with regard to abduction (see e.g. Hintikka 1998; Minnameier 2004; Paavola 2006; Campos 2011). This is in part due to the fact that Peirce changed his inferential theory significantly during the last decade of the 19th century, and even today many refer to the concepts of his previous approach.

The mature Peirce understands abduction as "the process of forming an explanatory hypothesis. It is the only logical operation which introduces any new idea" (1903/1965: 106 [CP 5.171]). "Explanation" in this context means to develop a theory to accommodate explanation seeking facts in a very broad sense. It can be a narrative account of certain puzzling facts like in a criminal case or a scientific theory. According to Peirce, however, "Abduction merely suggests that something *may be*. Its only justification is that from its suggestion deduction can draw a prediction which can be tested by induction" (ibid.).

As the quotation indicates, there is a natural succession of abduction, deduction, and induction, according to which abduction produces new ideas, deduction draws necessary consequences from them (and other background knowledge), and induction finally concerns the judgement whether the theory in question is to be accepted or rejected, or whether the matter has to remain open for the time being. Figure 1 illustrates this dynamical relationship.

Figure 1: Dynamic interaction of abduction, deduction, and induction

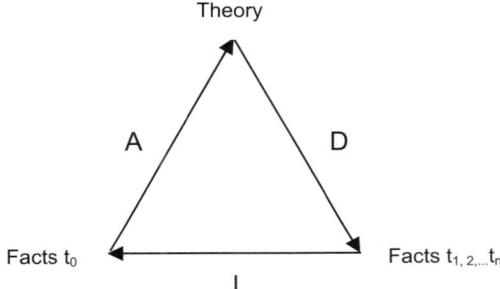

Source: own diagram

As already explained, abduction starts from surprising facts at t_0 and leads to a new concept or theory that accommodates those facts. From the theory and from suitable additional premises, consequences can be deduced. In particular, these can be empirical hypotheses about what is to be observed in experiments, if the theory is true. These expectations are the result of deduction. The deduced experiments carried out are the starting point for induction, where the actual experimental outcomes (facts at t_1 to t_n) have to be compared to the theoretical forecasts. These experimental results have to satisfy the mind that either the theory is to be accepted as true (based on the subject's current overall knowledge) or whether it has to be rejected as false. If true, the qualities stated by the theory are mapped onto the relevant cases, i.e. the original problem case, the tested cases, and all other past and future cases which the theory applies to. If false, the theory is said not to hold for all these cases.

This inductive projection from known cases to unknown cases also builds the bridge from knowledge acquisition to knowledge application and to future corroboration or refutation of the theory. Every new case to be encountered has to be first identified as a case of the theory (just like any concrete object has to be recognised and interpreted in terms of the category it represents). This is an abductive process in the application context. Next, deduction yields the corresponding action scheme, based also on the special conditions in the situation. If successful, the theory will be corroborated. If the action fails, the question arises as to whether the theory is false or whether the failure was due to certain side conditions. Deciding this question, again, is a matter of induction.

The validity of abduction, deduction, and induction: So far the three inferences have been described in their dynamical relationship. However, if all three are considered "logical" there has to be a criterion for each, according to which we can determine whether the inference is correct or incorrect. For deduction, we can say that the conclusion has to be implied by the premises so that the conclusion necessarily follows from them. But what are the criteria of logicality for abduction and induction?

Peirce himself propounds a strong notion of logicality for all three inferences:

> (W)hile Abductive and Inductive reasoning are utterly irreducible, either to the other or to Deduction, or Deduction to either of them, yet the only *rationale* of these methods is essentially Deductive or Necessary. If then we can state wherein the validity of Deductive reasoning lies, we shall have defined the foundation of logical goodness of whatever kind (1903/1965: 91 [CP 5.146]).

When Peirce says that abduction and induction are "essentially Deductive and Necessary", the stress must be on "essentially", for if they were equivalent to deduction, the argument of irreducibility would be false. The inconsistency on the surface vanishes with Peirce's explanation of what he means by *necessary* reasoning: A statement is "necessary", if it makes us see that what we perceive is of a general nature.

As far as abduction is concerned, the task is to accommodate the initial problematic facts (see 1903/1965: 122-123 [CP 5.197]) and to judge whether the new idea that has been generated in the process really does accommodate the facts. The "general nature" in this case is that, if we are not mistaken, we would always and in any similar case have to acknowledge that the theory does accommodate the facts. As Peirce says, any logical judgement implies some kind of surrender to the conclusion when we are satisfied that the respective criterion is met. "Now the surrender which we make in Retroduction[2], is a surrender to the insistence of an Idea" (1898/1965: 404 [CP 5.581]). However, the ability to accommodate the facts makes an account *possible*, though not necessarily in the sense that it must be true. Therefore, abductions have to be further explored by deduction and induction. Or to put it, once again, in Peirce's own words: "Deduction proves that something *must be*; Induction shows that something *actually is* operative; Abduction merely suggests that something *may be*" (1903/1965: 106 [CP 5.171]).

Peirce's notion of the abductive judgement is well known and goes like this:

> The surprising fact, C, is observed;
> But if A were true, C would be a matter of course,
> Hence, there is reason to suspect that A is true
> (1903/1965: 117 [CP 5.189]).

---

[2] "Retroduction" and "abduction" actually mean the same thing. They are simply two different labels for the same idea.

What the judgement tells us is no more and no less than that A explains C, and that this is necessarily so. It is easy to see that necessity of this kind does not imply any statement regarding the truth of A. Nor does it involve any claim of entailment in the deductive sense, for C does not entail A. It is only stated that A entails C, which is just the explanatory relation.[3]

Concerning the validity of the inductive judgement, Peirce points out that it basically consists in projecting the posited theoretical qualities onto all possible instances. He gives the example of an infinite series of symbols for which a certain pattern is assumed and examined, and for which a judgement as to its overall regularity is made on the basis of finite experience (see 1903/1965:105 [CP 5.170]). He concludes that "the validity of induction depends upon the necessary relation between the general and the singular" (ibid.).

Induction, therefore, is the inference that yields factual knowledge, constituting factual truth (whereas deduction only yields so-called logical truths and abduction merely plausible ideas). Now, what may be seen as problematic in this respect is the relation between knowledge and truth. The classical notion of knowledge as *justified true belief* requires that a proposition be true in order to be known. However, a main theorem from the point of view of pragmatism is that knowledge is logically prior, i.e. knowledge establishes truth rather than requiring it as a condition (concerning this shift compare e.g. the contextualist notion of knowledge; see e.g. DeRose 2009).

The same line is followed by F. Suppe (1997) when he suggests a non-reliabilistic externalist approach to knowledge. In this view, we know p when it is not causally possible (indicated by a causal possibility operator $\Diamond$)[4] that we perceive the evidence unless the suggested hypothesis is true. Without being able to set this out in detail here, this approach meets with the elaborated eliminative inductivism proposed by Earman (1992) and the notion of practical truth suggested by Da Costa and French (e.g. 2003) (see also Minnameier 2004). According to Suppe's approach, truth collapses with knowledge in a conscious act, which is described in condition (iv) below. And "satisfying (iv) entails the satisfaction of condition (iii)" (Suppe 1997: 402), since R and/or K function as decisive indicators for Φ.

---

3   As opposed to this, deduction aims at revealing further necessary consequences (new derivable statements) of the hypothetical statement of A together with premises from background knowledge. It should, however, also be noted that things are slightly different with respect to theorematic deduction – an issue which cannot be treated in the present paper (see Minnameier, 2005, pp. 195-218).

4   Causal possibility refers to all logically possible worlds consistent with the natural laws of our world.

S propositionally knows that θ if and only if
(i) *S* undergoes a cognitive process *R*, or *S* has prior knowledge that *K*;
(ii) *S*, knowing how to use Φ and knowing how to use θ with the same propositional intent, as a result of undergoing *R* or having prior knowledge that *K* entertains the proposition Φ with that propositional intent as being factually true or false;
(iii) 'Φ' is factually true;
(iv) there exists a conjunction *C* of partial world state descriptions and probability spaces such that *C* & ~◇^{Φ}(*C* & *R* & *K* & ~Φ) & ◇^{Φ}(*C* & ~Φ) & ◇*R* & ◊(*R* & ~Φ);
(v) as a result of undergoing *R* or *K*, *S* believes that Φ (Suppe 1997, p. 405).

Theory of science is not our concern here, but it should at least be mentioned that the above rationale might also work as a criterion for truth in the context of D. Mayo's concept of "severe testing" of theories (see Mayo 2010).

1.3 Mistakes: How to Get It Wrong

1.3.1 Inferential Processes

In order to determine the various mistakes that can be made we have to analyse the inferential process in some more detail. All inferences are mental acts of reasoning, and as such describe a process with a definite beginning and a definite end. According to Peirce the inferential process as such can – and supposedly has to – be subdivided into three distinct steps. These steps are "colligation", "observation", and "judgement" (for more detail on Peirce's view of the inferential process see Minnameier 2010a).

The first step of inference usually consists in bringing together certain propositions which we believe to be true, but which, supposing the inference to be a new one, we have hitherto not considered together, or not as united in the same way. This step is called colligation. (c. 1893/1974: 267-268 [CP 2.442])

The next step of inference to be considered consists in the contemplation of that complex icon ... so as to produce a new icon. (...) It thus appears that all knowledge comes to us by observation. A part is forced upon us from without and seems to result from Nature's mind; a part comes from the depths of the mind as seen from within ... (c. 1893/1974: 268-269 [CP 2.443-4])

A few mental experiments – or even a single one ... – satisfy the mind that the one icon would at all times involve the other, that is, suggest it in a special way ... Hence the mind is not only led from believing the premiss to judge the conclusion true,[5] but it further attaches to this judgment another – that every proposition like the premiss, that is having an icon like it, would involve, and compel acceptance of, a proposition related to it as the

---

5   The talk of "truth" here is certainly misleading, since the passage should apply to all three inferences. It would be more appropriate to speak of a "valid" inference.

conclusion then drawn is related to that premiss. [This is the third step of inference.] (c. 1893/1974: 268 [CP 2.444]).

He concludes that "(t)he three steps of inference are, then, colligation, observation, and the judgment that what we observe in the colligated data follows a rule" (c. 1893/1974: 269 [CP 2.444]). Put differently, colligation marks the beginning and preliminary work for an inference, observation refers to the searching process based on the colligated premise, and judgement determines whether the observed result yields a valid conclusion. In this process, observation covers the creative part of any inference, in which spontaneous ideas are produced not only in abduction, but also in deduction and induction (see Peirce 1898/1965: 404 [CP 5.581], c. 1893/1974: 268-269 [CP 2.443-4]). As opposed to this, judgement concerns the rational part of inference (see Peirce 1903/1965: 112-113 [CP 5.181]). This comes out nicely in a passage on deduction, where, however, Peirce speaks of "experiment", but quite obviously means "judgement" according to the terminology introduced here (see also Minnameier 2010a).

(We) begin a Deduction by writing down all the premises. Those different premises are then brought into one field of assertion, that is, are colligated ... Thereupon, we proceed attentively to observe the graph. It is just as much an operation of Observation as is the observation of bees. This observation leads us to make an experiment upon the Graph. Namely, we first duplicate portions of it; and then we erase portions of it, that is, we put out of sight part of the assertion to see what the rest of it is. We observe the result of this experiment, and that is our deductive conclusion. (1898/1965: 402 [CP 5.579])

Now, Peirce's reflections on the present issue mainly refer to deduction, so that it may be asked how these processes relate to abduction and induction. To be sure, Peirce mentions something in this respect, but is less explicit about the sub-processes (especially judgement) as far as abduction and induction are concerned. Nonetheless, I believe the revealed principles can be transferred in a fairly straightforward manner. The sub-processes of all three inferences are presented in technical form in Table 1 and explained below for abduction and induction.

Table 1: Formalisation of inferential processes

Inference:	Abduction	Deduction	Induction
Colligation:	C	$H \wedge P$	$\Box((H \wedge P) \rightarrow E) \wedge E$
Observation:	$H \rightarrow \Diamond C$	$(H \wedge P) \rightarrow E$	$E \wedge \neg \Diamond (E \wedge \neg H)$
Judgement:	$\Diamond H$	$\Box((H \wedge P) \rightarrow E)$	$\boxed{c}\, H$

Source: own table

As already mentioned above, abduction begins with a problem statement. This problem statement constitutes the premise on which abduction is based. More precisely, it contains all the relevant information on the case(s) to be explained or to be mastered in some way (e.g. technological problems in which a certain effect is to be produced).

The colligated premise is subsequently observed in the search for a (possible) solution. Any such solution will be generated spontaneously in the process of observation. In the judgemental phase, it is finally checked whether the observed result really accommodates the facts, i.e. whether it is "causally possible". This is indicated by the causal possibility operator $\diamondsuit$ (see Footnote 4). The chosen hypotheses or approaches are further examined by deduction and induction; the others are discarded.

The inductive inference consists of the deduced testing situation ($\square((H \wedge P) \rightarrow E)$) and its manifest result (E), i.e. the sensory or narrative record of what has actually happened. The evidence may also include (and sometimes exclusively consists of) relevant past experiences.[6] This result is observed in order to reveal confirming and disconfirming aspects (i.e. with respect to the target criterion mentioned in Table 1 and explicated at the end of Section 2). Eventually, the overall evidence is weighed and a judgement taken as to whether the theory in question is to be accepted or rejected, or whether the whole question is still pending. In the positive case, the evidence not only has to confirm the theory, but it is also required that it is not causally possible that the same evidence would also sanction another hypothesis ($\neg \diamondsuit (E \wedge \neg H)$). If this is the case, H is causally necessary ($\square H$).

1.3.2 Types of Mistakes

Following this rationale of inferential sub-processes, at least three different types of mistakes can be made within each inference: mistakes of colligation, mistakes of observation, and mistakes of judgement.

Mistakes of colligation consist in ignoring or misinterpreting relevant information in the premise. As for abduction, this concerns the initial problem statement. Here, for example, relevant information may be overlooked. As for deduction, the theory and the characteristics of the situation have to be restated, but also supplemented by relevant background knowledge. Again, relevant information might be omitted or misread. And similarly, colligation in the inductive context implies a restatement of the empirical hypotheses derived by deduction plus a complete and adequate representation of the actual results or relevant past experiences.

---

6 For instance, when companies engage in new markets or consider new strategies, they typically cannot test them beforehand in a real or simulated setting.

Mistakes of observation simply mean that no suitable result is generated in the inferential act. In the context of abduction, the subject fails to have a plausible idea of how to solve the problem. The same applies to deduction, where one fails to see what follows necessarily from the premises (but only with respect to relevant deductive consequences). Inductively, one would fail to produce relevant confirming or disconfirming evidence in an experiment.

Of course, one might always "observe", at first glance, something that is, and hopefully turns out to be, inferentially invalid – a stupid idea in the abductive context, for instance. However, such lapses would have to be noticed and eliminated in the judgemental sub-process.

Mistakes of judgement, thus, consist in failing to see that the observed inferential result is in fact invalid, when and wherever this is the case. And inferential invalidity means that a theory does not accommodate the facts (abduction), that the putative deductive conclusion is not entailed by the premises (deduction), or that the collected evidence does not warrant the inductive conclusion about the status of the theory. As for the latter, the evidence can be suited to confirm or refute a theory (at least for the time being), or it may turn out to be insufficient in determining the truth or falsity of the theory in question. Any decision in this respect that is not warranted by the evidence, codes for a judgemental mistake.

1.3.3 Example

Let us illustrate these processes with an example from accounting. The initial problem arises in an event that has to be registered in the accounting system. First the event – say something is bought – has to be understood as such and the information gathered, i.e. what it was, whether it was paid for right away and how, how much VAT is to be paid and so on. This is the process of colligation in the abductive context (any omission or misunderstanding would constitute a mistake in this respect). Starting from this colligation, the suitable accounts for these instances have to be found, i.e. the situation has to be reconstructed on an abstract level, first by observation, and if the subject has an idea, this idea has to pass muster of the abductive judgement, i.e. whether it would accommodate the colligated facts. Failing to generate such an approach would be an observational mistake. The failure to realise that it does not fit (if this is the case), would be a judgmental mistake.

Starting from the abduced approach, the respective entry formula must be deduced, i.e. the right booking on the accounts and the correct values have to be determined, beginning with the approach and the information from the case (colligation). Here, the failure to activate relevant accounting background knowledge would be a colligative mistake (presupposing that this knowledge exists, in principle) – e.g. on which sides to book. Observational mistakes mean that the right solution is not found and a judgmental mistake arises in not realising that the derived formula is false (i.e. not noticing that the result does not *necessarily* follow from the premises).

Induction starts with the deductive result and what this produces in the physical or the accounting reality. The latter would concern consequences for other accounts and whether these seem correct or incorrect. If a purchase leads to more rather than less cash assets, there must be a mistake somewhere. Collecting the information is the colligative, analysing it the observational and coming to a conclusion the judgmental part. Failing to notice a piece of information as indicated above is a mistake of colligation, failing to see its relevance is one of observation, and, for example, finding that this is strange but perhaps not false, is one of judgement.

It should be noted that, in educational contexts, teachers most often function as the inductive criterion. If the teacher says that the result is correct, this is considered as a decisive indicator. However, if the students could see for themselves if their result is correct or not, it might be justified to ascribe inductive reasoning mistakes of one of the three sorts, for failing to consider the information at hand. Therefore, teachers should perhaps not immediately answer such questions, but ask students to make up their own minds.

1.4 Errors: How to be Right and Still Go Wrong

Peter Achinstein (2004: 13-17) discusses a useful real-world example of failures that are the outcome of correct and even very intelligent and learned reasoning. It is about the theoretical explanation of cathode rays.

Cathode rays were discovered in 1859 by Julius Plücker, who noticed that the glass near the cathode in a tube glows with a greenish phosphorescence, when a source with high electrical potential is connected to the anode and the tube and the air pressure in the tube is sufficiently reduced. One of his students also noticed that those cathode rays cast shadows just as light does. The ensuing theoretical question was whether to explain cathode rays either as negatively charged particles or as waves. Heinrich Hertz, who belonged to the wave-theorists, conducted experiments to determine whether cathode rays are electrically charged and whether they are affected by external electrostatic forces. According to the wave theory neither should be the case.

In his carefully planned experiments (described in ibid.: 14-15) he found evidence for his hypotheses and concluded that "(t)hese cathode rays are electrically indifferent, and amongst known agents the phenomenon most nearly allied to them is light" (Hertz 1896: 254, quoted from Achinstein 2004: 15).

However, Hertz was wrong. What he did not know was that the electrical charge of cathode rays, which really exists, was neutralised by the rarefied gas in the tube. When J. J. Thomson conducted suitably modified experiments in 1897, i.e. 14 years after Hertz's, he discovered both the electrical charge of the cathode rays and their susceptibility to external electrostatic forces, which resulted in a deflection of the rays.

Hence, Hertz was clearly wrong. However, has he made any mistake? The crucial question here is whether he could have known, or at least should have considered, that the tube was not sufficiently evacuated. We know that Hertz himself was, at his time, not yet able to evacuate the air from the tube to the extent that he could ever have observed the effect that disproved his theory. Had he had the means, he would certainly have attained the correct experimental results and would have come to the correct conclusion.

Nonetheless, Hertz might perhaps have thought of the possibility that the tube was not sufficiently evacuated to permit the rays to be electrically deflected, should they be charged. In this case, he could, on the one hand, have concluded, as he did, that "under the conditions of the experiment the cathode rays were not deflected by an electromotive force existing in the space traversed by them" (1896: 253, quoted from Achinstein 2004: 15). But on the other hand, he would have had to qualify also his final conclusion and make clear that his judgement depended on the precondition that complete vacuum does not make any difference (even though he himself could not probe for it).

Thus, if Hertz could have thought of this possibility, he clearly made a mistake, in this case an inductive one. He would have had to consider this aspect in the course of inductively observing his experimental results and, as a consequence, would have come to a different inductive judgement. If, however, he could not have thought of it, or if there was no reason whatsoever for him to consider this aspect, we could call it an error, where "error" is defined as a failure which the epistemic subject is not to be accounted for.

1.5 Instruction and Construction: How to Get It Right

The results for educational interventions can only be summarised in a cursory manner here (however, see also the contribution by Maxi Link in the present volume, where instructional strategies to deal with mistakes are elaborated). Error- or mistake-based instruction requires, first of all, a proper diagnosis of the failures to be addressed. Teachers have to work out where exactly their students go wrong and point to the respective issues with suitable prompts. If they were not sure about the exact nature of a mistake, teachers could simply start with the first (sub-)process in the reasoning chain to see how long the students remain with them and where their thinking goes astray.

With respect to errors, teachers will have to create situations that reveal the flaws to their students, i.e. they have to contrive decisive experiments (which may also be thought experiments). The classical and perhaps most important forms of error are those which are due to inappropriate or immature cognitive structures in Piaget's sense. Consider a child that does not know or refuses to accept that the earth is round. One experiment to prove him or her wrong would be to make them watch ships approaching the shore. The first thing one makes out is the mast or the sail (or the chimney of a steamer). If the earth were flat, you ought to see the ship as a whole (though very small). However, you always see the top first and only later the hull appears. This refutes the view that the earth is flat and confirms that it must be curved.

Another form of failure that we have not addressed, but which is also important in the educational context, relates to the *execution* of a plan, i.e. to its *enactment*. For instance, when a child is learning to whistle, knows what to do and thus has a correct plan (both verbalised and from watching a suitable model), but still does not succeed in whistling owing to the subtleties of the activity.[7] This kind of failure points to the problem that knowledge at a given level of reasoning has to be *transformed* into an action at a lower level, which involves a kind of leap from the higher to the lower level. Theory can guide practice, but it is neither equivalent to it (not even in part), nor can the former replace the latter.

Whether the unsuccessful enactment of a (correct) plan is to be regarded as a mistake or as an error depends, again, on whether the subject can or cannot be accounted for the failure. However, this issue would have to be analysed in the context of another inferential triad *on the lower level* – in this case on the level of perceptual or enactive judgements.[8]

As for appropriate interventions, executional failures are avoided or cured mainly by training and experience. Mental training might support the shift from theory to practice. Sometimes, further reflection and a resulting refinement of the plan could also be an option.

At any rate, inferential processes *on a certain level of functioning* and transformations *across levels* are not to be confounded and must be clearly

---

[7] It has to be noted that such failures are not equivalent with either of what J. Reason calls "slips" and "lapses" (see e.g. 1990: 9). "Slips" are explained as executional, but at the same time, slips are conceived of as happening by chance rather than systematically. However, executional failures, like the one in the whistling example, can indeed be very systematic and persisting. "Lapses", by contrast, are associated with memory or attentional deficiencies, which in the present framework can be reconstructed as *either* mistakes of colligation (failing to consider available information or background knowledge) *or* mistakes of observation (failing to see something more or less obvious) or a mistake of judgement (failing to spot and reject a faulty observation).

[8] For the question of how far sensual perception can be reconstructed in terms of abduction, deduction, and induction see Minnameier (2010a). A perceptual judgement pertains to believing what one perceives, an enactive judgement to the perceived quality of an act.

distinguished in the analysis of cognitive and behavioural adaptation in general, and learning from mistakes and errors in particular.

References

Achinstein, P. (2004): *The book of evidence*, 2nd edn., New York: Oxford University Press.
Campos, D.G. (2011): On the distinction between Peirce's abduction and Lipton's inference to the best explanation. In: *Synthese*, 180, pp. 419-442.
Cannon, M.D./Edmondson, A.C. (2005): Failing to learn and learning to fail (intelligently): How great organizations put failure to work to improve and innovate. In: *Long Range Planning: International Journal of Strategic Management* 38, 3, pp. 299-319.
Copi, I.M./Cohen, C. (2004): *Introduction to logic*, 2nd edn., Englewood Cliffs, NJ: Prentice Hall.
Da Costa, N.C.A./French, S. (2003): *Science and partial truth: A unitary approach to models and scientific reasoning*. Oxford: Oxford University Press.
DeRose, K. (2009): *The case for contextualism: Knowledge, skepticism, and context, Vol. 1*. Oxford: Oxford University Press.
Dörner, D./Schaub, H. (1994): Errors in planning and decision-making and the nature of human information processing. In: *Applied Psychology*, 43, 4, pp. 433-453.
Earman, J. (1992): *Bayes or bust? A critical examination of Bayesian confirmation theory*, Cambridge, MA: MIT Press.
Gabbay, D.M./Woods, J. (2005): *A practical logic of cognitive systems, Vol. 2: The reach of abduction – insight and trial*. Amsterdam: Elsevier.
Gardner, Martin (2001): A skeptical look at Karl Popper. In: *Skeptical Inquirer*, 25, 4, pp. 13-14, 72.
Gartmeier, M./Bauer, J./Gruber, H./Heid, H. (2008): Negative knowledge: Understanding professional learning and expertise. In: *Vocations and Learning*, 1, 2, pp. 87-103.
Harteis, C./Bauer, J./Gruber, H. (2008): The culture of learning from mistakes: How employees handle mistakes in everyday work. In: *International Journal of Educational Research*, 47, 4, pp. 223-231.
Hertz, H. (1896): *Miscellaneous Papers*. London: Macmillan.
Hintikka, J. (1998): What is abduction? The fundamental problem of contemporary epistemology. In: *Transactions of the Charles S. Peirce Society*, 34, 3, pp. 503-533.
Ludquist, R. (1999): Critical thinking and the art of making good mistakes. In: *Teaching in Higher Education*, 4, 4, pp. 523-530.
Magnani, L. (2009): *Abductive cognition: The epistemological and eco-cognitive dimensions of hypothetical reasoning*. Berlin: Springer.
Mayo, D.G. (2010): Learning from error, severe testing, and the growth of theoretical knowledge. In: Mayo, D.G./Spanos, A. (eds.): *Error and inference: Recent ex-*

changes on experimental reasoning, reliabilitiy, and the objectivity and rationality of science. New York: Cambridge University Press, pp. 28-57.

Meyer, L./Seidel, T./Prenzel, M. (2006): Wenn Lernsituationen zu Leistungssituation werden: Untersuchungen zur Fehlerkultur in einer Videostudie. In: *Schweizerische Zeitschrift für Bildungswissenschaften*, 28, 1, pp. 21-41.

Minnameier, G. (2004): Peirce-suit of truth: Why inference to the best explanation and abduction ought not to be confused. In: *Erkenntnis*, 60, pp. 75-105.

Minnameier, G. (2005): *Wissen und inferentielles Denken: Zur Analyse und Gestaltung von Lehr-Lern-Prozessen.* Frankfurt/Main: Lang.

Minnameier, G. (2010a): The logicality of abduction, deduction, and induction. In: Bergman, M./Paavola, S./Pietarinen, A.-V./Rydenfelt, H. (eds.): *Ideas in action: Procedures of the Applying Peirce conference.* Helsinki: Nordic Pragmatism Network, pp. 216-228. (http://www.nordprag.org/nsp/1/Minnameier.pdf)

Minnameier, G. (2010b): Abduction, induction, and analogy – On the compound character of analogical inferences. In: Carnielli, W./Magnani, L./Pizzi, C. (eds.): *Model-based reasoning in science and technology: Abduction, logic, and computational discovery.* Heidelberg: Springer, pp. 107-119.

Oser, F./Spychiger, M. (2005): *Lernen ist schmerzhaft: Zur Theorie des Negativen Wissens und zur Praxis der Fehlerkultur.* Basel: Beltz.

Paavola, S. (2006): Hansonian and harmanian abduction as models of discovery. In: *International Studies in the Philosophy of Science*, 20, 1, pp. 93-108.

Peirce, C.S. (1898/1965): Methods for attaining truth. In: Hartshorne, C./Weiss, P. (eds.): *The collected papers of Charles Sanders Peirce, Vol. V: Pragmatism and pragmaticism.* Cambridge, MA: The Belknap Press, pp. 399-422.

Peirce, C.S. (1902/1974): Why study logic? In: Hartshorne, C./Weiss, P. (eds.): *The collected papers of Charles Sanders Peirce, Vol. II: Elements of logic.* Cambridge, MA: The Belknap Press, pp. 67-125.

Peirce, C.S. (1903/1965): Lectures on pragmatism. In: Hartshorne, C./Weiss, P. (eds.): *The collected papers of Charles Sanders Peirce, Vol. V: Pragmatism and pragmaticism.* Cambridge, MA: The Belknap Press, pp. 13-131.

Peirce, C.S. (c. 1893/1974): The grammatical theory of judgement and inference. In Hartshorne, C./Weiss, P. (eds.): *The collected papers of Charles Sanders Peirce, Vol. II: Elements of logic.* Cambridge, MA: The Belknap Press, pp. 265-269.

Rasmussen, J. (1980): What can be learned from human error reports? In: Duncan, K./ Gruneberg, M./Wallis, D. (eds.): *Changes in working life.* London: Wiley, pp. 97-113.

Reason, J. (1987): Generic error-modelling system (GEMS): A cognitive framework for locating common human error forms. In: Rasmussen, J./Duncan, K./Leplat, J. (eds.): *New Technology and human error.* New York: Wiley & Sons, pp. 63-83.

Reason, J. (1990): *Human error.* Cambridge: Cambridge University Press.

Seifried, J./Wuttke, E. (2010): Potenziale des Lernens aus Fehlern in Abhängigkeit von methodischen Grundentscheidungen. In: Seifried, J./Wuttke, E./Nickolaus, R./Sloane, P. F. E. (eds.): *Lehr-Lern-Forschung in der kaufmännischen Berufsbildung – Ergebnisse und Gestaltungsaufgaben.* Stuttgart: Steiner, pp. 155-171.

Suppe, F. (1997): Science without induction. In: Earman, J./Norton, J. D. (eds.): *The cosmos of science: Essays of exploration.* Pittsburgh, PA: University of Pittsburgh Press, pp. 386–429.

Weingardt, M. (2004): *Fehler zeichnen uns aus. Transdisziplinäre Grundlagen zur Theorie und Produktivität des Fehlers in Schule und Arbeitswelt.* Bad Heilbrunn: Klinkhardt.
Yerushalmi, E./Polingher, C. (2006): Guiding students to learn from mistakes. In: *Physics Education,* 41, 6, pp. 532-537.

2 Learning from Mistakes – Still a Challenge for Research and Business Practice

Christian Harteis and Katrin Buschmeyer

2.1 Introduction

Daily life regularly proves human fallibility in manifold ways. Everybody's daily experiences deviate from the intended goals of actions, at least in simple ways. For instance, in computer software that does not work as expected, in news concerning incidents in which individuals committed big mistakes causing accidents, or in stories about complex systems that failed due to unexpected events meeting with insufficient equipment (e.g. problem in the German public transportation system). Additionally, everybody remembers an incident in which they commited a mistake due to lack of attention (e.g. replying a forwarded email not to the intended person but to the sender). Daily life is accompanied by manifold mistakes of various qualities and reasons – nobody denies the sayings: "nobody's perfect" and "to err is human". However, not all mistakes end in catastrophes or with unpleasant results. Mistakes may also end in improvement and new inventions. Biological evolution is a matter of deviant genetic equipment, which proves to outclass the previous equipment. The Bavarian Pretzel is also supposed to be a product of a mistake: In 1839, the baker Anton Nepomuk mixed up sugared water and caustic lye of soda (which is toxic) during the preparation of the batter and didn't realise his mistake – as legend has it – not before having put them into the oven. He baked them and was positively surprised about the golden-brown delicious result of his mistake. Today, the Pretzel is a world-famous example of development caused by learning from a mistake.

In positive cases, the results of mistakes provide further advantages to those who made the mistakes. These cases indicate the importance of mistakes for development. Negative cases of accidents causing unpleasant effects (e.g. the melting of the reactor at Chernobyl) indicate the necessity to learn from mistakes because it is important to avoid their repetition. However, as learning from mistakes is so important, it might be surprising that this issue is still a challenge to researchers as well as to practitioners. This article explores the issue of learning from mistakes by providing an explanation for the slow development of research and organisational interests and by reflecting, so far, on unsolved problems in theory and practice.

2.2 Mistakes and Business Organisation

During the history of research on business organisation, mistakes always had certain relevance, but the judgement of these mistakes (and their value) developed different shapes. Taylor (1939/1911) may have marked the starting point of research on business organisation when he wrote his seminal work on scientific management. His goal was to specify the inhouse processes in a shape which optimizes outcomes and productivity by precisely describing working steps as simply as possible. The idea was to avoid mistakes by precisely describing processes which are simple and, thus, easier for workers to follow. Taylor's development of managerial rationalism influenced Ford's (2007/1922) invention of the assembly line production and made mass production of his car – the T-Model – possible. The main advantage of a scientific arrangement of belt production was its efficacy to produce huge masses of identical products, which are appropriate for a "lowly-saturated market".

In both ideas of business organisation, a strict fragmentation and standardisation of procedures as well as the consequent distinction and separation of planning work tasks and executing work tasks shaped the enterprises' organisational structures (Slattery 2003). As a result, those who planned working processes were supposed to design optimal processes of work division. Those who executed these processes were expected to follow exactly the prescriptions. For both approaches, mistakes were to be considered as disturbing incidents which were dangerous for the enterprise's productivity. Mistakes were, hence, to be avoided – they were not allowed to occur at all. Mistakes indicated inadequate work performance – either while planning or executing steps. In this strict separation between planning and work execution, learning from mistakes was not seen as an issue of relevance for the organisation.

More recent literature mainly focuses on the globalization and hard competition in the market, and suggests newly arising challenges for business organisation (Baud/Garrick 1999). It emphasizes learning as the crucial aspect of business organisation to fulfill future demands. Enterprises have to face the globalization of the markets with flexibility and innovative structures. At the very least, they are forced to react to permanently changing environments shaped by customers' demands and competitors' behaviours. It is particularly the fast development of the tertiary industrial sector which focuses more on employees and their skills, adaption potential and flexibility (Tennant 1999). Hence, learning processes became an important issue to face the intensified economic competition.

A twofold change occurred in the 1990s: (1) As workers were considered as individuals, they became a resource for the enterprises and for business organisations. (2) With increasing complexity of products, technology, knowledge, business structures, and market conditions, the insight was established that mistakes cannot be totally avoided.

The logical consequence was that workers became human resources of business management in order to improve products or processes and to identify mistakes in order to deduce consequences. It was the Toyota strategy of Kaizen (Imai 1986) which aimed at a permanent reflection of practices and procedures. This concept particularly addressed the workers at the operational level and not just the planning units of an enterprise. It overcame the separation between planning (thinking) and executing (doing) tasks by declaring that all workers are responsible for the quality of the business organisation. These approaches of business organisation (perhaps implicitly) accepted mistakes as, for the most part, unavoidable parts of complex working procedures. All members of an enterprise were expected to be aware of these approaches in order to work on process and product quality.

The latest approaches toward business organisation finally claimed that learning processes are crucial aspects of business activities (e.g., Argyris 1999, Senge 1994): The broad use of terms such as learning organisation, knowledge-based enterprise, and competence-based enterprise indicate this concern for learning processes in business management. Key components of these approaches comprise (at least in this sense) a permanent reflection of processes practiced within an enterprise – the core idea of ISO certification is a reflection of the practices in order to maintain reasonable structures and eliminate irrational ones – and continuous learning and individual development of the entire staff. The acknowledgement of the unavoidability of mistakes implies a consideration of the ambiguity of mistakes. On the one hand, the quality of processes and products should be error-free. On the other hand, as we all know from various areas of life, even good products or processes may fail. The evaluation of mistakes is thus ambiguous: They are to be avoided, but if they occur, they are to be seen as opportunities for learning and improvement – particularly when it is assumed that they cannot be totally avoided.

During the development of several generations of business organisations, mistakes have therefore been considered more or less explicitly as inevitable parts of organisational occurrences within enterprises. However, neither literature on business management nor literature on human resource development or business education reflects mistakes and learning from mistakes deeply. A theoretical description and an empirical foundation of an appropriate culture of learning from mistakes are still lacking, as the following exemplary review of literature reveals:

- Based on cybernetics and system theory, literature on organisational development, while acknowledging that mistakes are inevitable, does not provide precise strategies on how to utilise mistakes effectively (Kühl 2000). Cybernetic theories address the issue that deviances are necessary

for the improvement of a complex organism by referring to biological evolution. However, they do not provide concrete advice on how best to make use of mistakes, they rather occur and yield consequences identified as developments (e.g. Vester 2002).
- Research on organisational learning should be the major area for discussing learning from mistakes in business life. However, as the comprehensive literature review presented by Appelbaum and Gallagher (2000) reveals, mistakes are taken into consideration rather incidentally but without any theoretical underpinning. This deficit is not yet remedied in more recent literature (e.g. Glendon/Clarke/McKenna 2006).
- In the area of business literature, personnel development might be the most popular domain considering issues of learning and individual development. Literature on personnel development describes (a) from an individual perspective, strategies and approaches on how to best prepare for the professional career and (b) from an organisational perspective, the best way to arrange career planning and training interventions in order to meet an enterprise's demands. It is remarkable that this kind of literature, if mistakes are considered at all, exclusively focuses on mistakes as reversal points of aspiring careers and as jeopardising for an individual's progress. In Graupner's (2001) understanding, committing or admitting a mistake means a downturn in one's career. Hence, any failure must be avoided in order to avoid risking a successful career.
- Management literature considers mistakes mainly in the context of the issue concerning quality assurance. It was Toyota's idea of total quality management, having invented zero-mistake-strategies, which survived in recent business practices (e.g. the ISO certification). Mistakes are at the very least considered here as a starting point for improvement processes. However, theories on how to learn from such mistakes are not provided (Appelbaum/Gallagher 2000).

Considering the fact that the insight into the inevitability of mistakes is quite an old one and that literature – also on educational research – so far has not provided the theoretical underpinning and empirical evidence on learning from mistakes in business contexts, this contribution seeks to provide possible explanations for this deficit.

2.3 Explanations

The lack of a theoretical and empirical basis for learning from mistakes in daily business life may be explained either by the contradictory role of mistakes – as fruitful material for learning but as disruptive events in the production process – or by three different problems of precisely developing a theoretical construction of mistakes. The following paragraphs will briefly discuss these issues.

2.3.1 The Role of Mistakes

Learning from mistakes in daily business life is a challenging issue, since mistakes still have quite a negative reputation. People who pursue a high level of performance usually try to avoid mistakes, as mistakes limit the quality of work performance. Working life in daily business, particularly if it is highly competitive, usually focuses on and rewards positive examples of work performance. Hence, mistakes do not appear to promote success in business and work life. That might explain the fact that literature on personal development mentions mistakes merely as examples of the disruption of an ambitious career. Educational researchers on learning from mistakes should not ignore or hide this characteristic of mistakes. Even though mistakes may bear opportunities for learning and improvement, they remain awkward events, at least for the agents and probably for an entire working group or enterprise.

It is an unchallenged task of management and business literature to provide approaches to and concepts for organising a successful business. Hence, productivity of processes is primarily considered. Learning purposes – necessarily – play at best a secondary role. Learning issues find consideration as long as they (immediately) support the business goals of productivity. Since mistakes interfere with productivity, they find consideration only in that respect – how to best avoid and eliminate mistakes. Learning from mistakes does not fall into the focus of reflection in this particular literature. The distinction between learning purposes and efficiency purposes is crucial here: Management and business organisation literature particularly focuses on business performance and, thus, follows considerations of efficiency of work processes. Hence, it is not surprising that learning from mistakes – clearly an issue of learning purposes – is not well considered in management and business organisation theories.

However, the question arises as to why educational and psychological literature also poorly reports research on learning from mistakes in business life. Oser and Spychiger (2005) conclude that mistakes are also negatively attributed to educational contexts. In their comprehensive book, which summarises their theoretical and empirical work on learning from mistakes from several years, they focus on school contexts. They work through various examples of negative attributions towards mistakes – even in contexts which are explicitly and exclusively designed for learning purposes. Learning purposes are, however, not considered a priority in business contexts, thus it cannot be cited as evidence for the lack of theoretical or empirical foundation of learning from mistakes in educational and psychological research. The problem might be related to the subjective mental attitude towards learning – e.g. an individual's error orientation (Rybowiak/Garst/Frese/Batinic 1999). This means that individual attitudes towards mistakes may impede the opportunities for learning from mistakes. As long as learning, in societal perception, is regarded as an error-free process or action, learning from mistakes might negatively affect an individual's reputation. Societal perception of learning implies faultlessness and mistakes disappear from public awareness, because only high achievement earns recognition. As Oser and Spychiger (2005) already claim, this kind of reward system for learning starts for children in the early years of school. The children receive grades to underline their learning achievements.

Researchers attempting to empirically investigate learning from mistakes in business life have to conquer the barrier of managements' scepticism towards research issues not (directly or obviously) supporting business efficiency. Educational and psychological researchers who are aiming at the investigation of learning from mistakes and are interested in issues which interrupt and interfere with the efficiency of business processes may face big challenges in conducting this kind of research. In any case, published empirical research describes these kinds of challenges as either participants or the management indicating resistance towards broaching the issue of mistakes in business life (van Dyck/Frese/Baer/Sonnentag 2005). Hence, the negative attribution of mistakes in educational contexts on the one hand and the barrier of individual or collective resistance against mistakes in business contexts on the other hand may explain the fact that there is no huge amount of educational and psychological literature on learning from mistakes in business life.

2.3.2 The Fuzziness of the Object of a Mistake

At first glance, it may appear simple and clear *what* a mistake is. One can follow, for example, Oser, Hascher, and Spychiger (1999), who define a mistake quite generally as a circumstance or process, which deviates from one or several norms. However, this definition alone does not clearly describe the object of a mistake but rather it generally introduces the idea of deviation as the main feature of a mistake. Therefore, this definition covers circumstances, as well as processes, which can deviate from norms. Hence, there is an additional component necessary: An observer who declares circumstances or processes as mistakes. For the clarification of the declaration of mistakes, it is necessary to precisely describe the object which deviates from norms. If – for example – a damaged car leaves the production line of a car manufacturer's plant, several mistakes could be possible: The damaged car itself, processes of insufficient quality, the execution of wrong work steps, or wrong decisions at certain points of the production process.

Possible learning from this mistake requires the clarification of what exactly the object of the mistake is. This simple example already reveals that the specification of the object of a mistake is not at all clear and simple. Each individual observation of a circumstance or process considers just a particular selective view of the real circumstance or process by distinguishing relevant information, which is intended for further consideration, and irrelevant information, which is then rejected. Several persons' views on circumstances or processes may differ widely. Hence, one has to acknowledge that the description of an object of a mistake might be different among several persons. The description of the object of a mistake is therefore neither simple nor clear at all.

The attempt to clearly describe what exactly a mistake is has so far revealed a certain fuzziness which appears difficult to resolve, as people may vary in their individual views on an object of a mistake. However, it becomes fuzzier if acknowledging that the absence of an action can also be regarded as a mistake. Not assisting/helping a person in danger is an obvious example of this kind of mistake. Hence, it becomes very obvious that the declaration of a mistake does not necessarily correspond to objects or procedures of physical nature (Reason 1990). For each circumstance or process of observation, an infinite number of possibly deferred actions can be construed. It is particularly crucial for the observation of a circumstance that not acting must also be considered for the determination of a mistake.

To sum up this paragraph: On the *level of content* – i.e. what exactly can be called a mistake – processes as well as circumstances arise as possible objects of mistakes. However, omitted actions can also be considered mistakes. Finally, the attribution of mistakes is always based on an individual's selective observation. Thus, judgments may vary among individuals.

2.3.3 Challenges of Judgment

As the declaration of mistakes is an attribution process, the moment of judgment enters the scope of reflection. The definition by Oser, Hascher, and Spychiger (1999) explicitly addresses the normative criterion for the judgment of a mistake. Declaring something as a mistake implies a deviance from a status, which the attributor considers as reference. In other words: An attributor judges a current state of an object of observation (i.e. circumstance, process, omitted action) as a deviation from (usually worse than) an intended standard. Hence, mistakes are an evaluative category. The attribution of a mistake implies that the attributor addresses a reference system and judges an object of observation on the basis of normative standards emerging from this reference system. In order to enhance learning from mistakes, the normative basis for the judgment of mistakes has to be transparent. Each choice of a reference system implies a selection process. This selection includes those norms of the chosen reference system and neglects those which describe different norms. Using the example of the damaged car, several norms are available to attribute the mistake: Producing quality (i.e. the damaged car itself as a mistake), working effectively (i.e. insufficient quality as a mistake), working correctly (i.e. wrong work steps as mistakes), and working well (i.e. wrong decisions as mistakes). It is inevitably necessary that those who are supposed to learn from this mistake must know which of these norms apply to the attribution of the mistake. This point of view raises several challenges:

Firstly, as enterprises comprise many people with different statuses and power, the following question arises: Who would be the appropriate person to decide the selection of the effective reference system? In hierarchical organisations – which might be the case in most enterprises – superiors usually evaluate the work performance of their working group. However, many enterprises are comprised of several hierarchical levels and several departments for a specific purpose. It seems to offer the people from different levels or departments the possibility to apply different norms according to their judgments. Referring to the damaged car, it seems plausible that persons at the production floor apply norms which are different from the norms applied in quality assurance when facing the mistake that a damaged car has left the plant. The inhouse hierarchy, and, perhaps, a person's individual competence provides the basis in assigning appropriate persons for the decision about effective reference systems.

Secondly, the challenge arises as to whether the selection of the effective reference system is taken for granted and whether all people (i.e. failing person, observing person, those who are supposed to learn from an incident) concerned about the issue of learning from mistakes share the same criteria. This challenge is threefold: (a) It might be possible that the person who committed a mistake followed norms different from those followed by the person who attributes the mistake. Further, it is conceivable that the person who attributes the mistake applies norms different from those applied by the people who are supposed to learn from an incident. It is also possible that a norm is first determined after a mistake occurred. (b) If different people apply different norms, it is also possible that people are not aware of the fact that they apply different norms. (c) In addition, it is possible that some of the people concerned do not agree with the effective judgement of a mistake.

However, in all cases, agreement would be important for developing an understanding of the mistake, an understanding of the situation that somebody failed in, and the motivation to learn from such an incident (i.e. to avoid the same mistake in the future).

Thirdly, normative rules underlying everyday work practices are not always explicitly explained and reflected. It is rather probable that they are negotiated, established, and transmitted by partly unconscious socialisation processes within an organisation and within working groups. By acknowledging this fact, it appears possible that people are not necessarily able to precisely describe the norms they are applying for the judgment of a mistake. However, for the development of an understanding within the concept of a "mistake", a precise description of evaluation criteria is unavoidable.

Summing-up: The attribution of mistakes is a result of a judgment which implies the selection of a normative reference system. Challenges arise from the issues of who decides about the application of which norms, and how concerned parties agree with the effective norms. Agreement on these issues is crucial for supporting learning from mistakes.

2.3.4 Effects of Mistakes

Considering the discussion of issues related to the declaration of events as mistakes, learning from mistakes also directly depends on the effects of mistakes. The most expensive and least effective way of dealing with mistakes is to hide or simply ignore them. Hence, enterprises should develop a standard way of dealing contructively with mistakes. This is a kind of handling of mistake situations which can be called a culture of dealing with mistakes. As long as the effects of mistakes – in the sense of dealing with mistakes – are foreseeable, the risk of neglecting mistakes should be low. This issue has an organisational and a personal component.

The organisational component reflects inhouse practices of social behaviour in a twofold manner. Firstly, there is the issue of general attitude towards mistakes. Literature discusses the issue of error orientation (Rybowiak et al. 1999; Bauer/Festner/Harteis/Heid/Gruber 2004), which represents the tendency either to accept mistakes as unavoidable – and thus as opportunities to improve – or to regard mistakes as events which have to be avoided in any case. Even though this concept is mainly used for individual attributions, it can be easily transferred to a social aggregate. The more an organisation tends to understand mistakes as unpleasant but unavoidable incidents, and as long as the practices of social behaviour within an organisation reflect this opinion, the less they risk an individual experiencing a sustained negative response in admitting a mistake and making it public. For organisational performance and creativity, the fear of mistakes prompts individuals to act more defensively and focus on well-established routines. There is empirical evidence that under such circumstances, organisational performance and especially group creativity is limited (e.g. Baer/Frese 2003). Hence, a learning oriented and socially shared attitude towards mistakes can be considered as a positive influence on learning from mistakes. Secondly, a cooperative method of social behaviour supports a common sharing of mistakes, whereas a very competitive method of social behaviour provokes individuals not to share their mistake experiences (van Dyck/Frese/Baer/Sonnentag 2005). A competitive method of social behaviour also tends to blame the individual who made or committed the mistake.

The individual component primarily refers to mental and emotional effects of mistakes. Oser and colleagues mention the individual awareness of being the initial cause of a failing incident as a crucial prerequisite for learning from mistakes (Oser/Spychiger 2005). An individual has to be aware of the mistake and has to realise that he or she is responsible for the mistake. Neither are trivial within the context of business organisation. If there is a high degree of division of labour, the mistake may not be obvious to the person who made the mistake but to somebody in a subsequent work step. In this case, the person who committed the mistake might not get feedback on his or her failing. Additionally, if an individual tends to attribute mistakes externally, the necessity to learn from mistakes individually might appear low. Bauer (2008) distinguished several clusters of individual methods of dealing with mistakes in nursery domains. In his study it became obvious that the majority of individuals show tendencies which appear unpromising for learning from mistakes. As mentioned above, enterprises face manifold challenges. The importance of learning from mistakes for business organisation is particularly noticeable when mistakes result in disasters. Hidden or neglected mistakes can be considered merely as an unused learning opportunity, but they can also develop into catastrophes if continuously ignored.

Nowadays, the management of mistakes of an organisation is accompanied by dilemmas. On the one hand, mistakes can interrupt the processes of the organisation and impede efficient planning and working. Hence, mistakes should be avoided whenever possible. On the other hand, mistakes can be the starting point of positive development and can help increase work quality in the long-term. However, this implies a positive climate for learning from mistakes. An effective error management therefore is one which supports both learning from and avoiding mistakes at the same time. The best avoidance of mistakes includes a method of dealing with (unavoidable) mistakes which maximizes the probability of learning from mistakes.

Finally, from an ethical point of view, several issues emerge, even in an open climate, where mistakes are seen as opportunities for the individual and organisational learning processes to take place. No one would deny that accumulating mistakes can negatively affect the reputation of the employee. Even if a mistake is declared as a learning situation for the employee who committed it, that does not mean that his mistake does not end up in an implicit assessment situation by the management. It is possible that the management would not agree in excluding this mistake or the faulty action and the learning situation of the employee in a further assessment of the situation. It is also possible that the faulty action could affect future assessment decisions concerning the employee. The situation mentioned above refers to the difference between what is said and what is thought by the people involved.

Is it possible - considering an individual's perspective – to strictly separate learning and assessment situations? As we all know, an evaluation of one's fellow comes naturally and, most of the time, it is unconscious. An organisation pretending to claim that all mistakes are seen as an opportunity to learn must make the staff and manager aware of the reality that the mistakes committed during the learning situation can possibly affect the overall assessment of the employees who committed the mistake.

Another aspect should be taken into consideration – to what extent does the original intention of the failing person, as well as his or her capabilities, influence the effects of a mistake for an individual? It is an educational problem to determine a person's responsibility for their actions if the demands overwhelm the person's capabilities. Furthermore, it is a crucial educational demand, at least, to consider a person's intention for the judgment of his or her behaviour (Heid 1991). These issues refer to elaborations on ethics of conviction and ethics of responsibility (Enderle 2007).

2.4 State of Educational Research

Within educational research, some theoretical and empirical approaches have been developed in order to understand learning from mistakes. Whereas Reason, Edmondson, and Rybowiak and colleagues investigated particular psychological aspects of dealing with mistakes, it was the working group of Oser from Fribourg which intended to approach the issue from an educational viewpoint. Their major contribution to learning from mistakes is the definition of the following prerequisites to individual learning from mistakes (Oser/Spychiger 2005):

1. The first and most important issue is to pause for a moment after the faulty action is recognised. It must not happen that the individual merely continues the process – he must rather stop in order to have the opportunity to cognitively recognise that a mistake occurred.
2. There must be feedback that a mistake occurred. As mentioned above, this is not self-evident, especially in organisations with high levels of division of labour. However, feedback is necessary in order to inform the individual about the mistake. There is no specified form of feedback considered but simply the notification of its occurrence.
3. In a sequence of interruption and feedback, the individual has to develop concern for the mistake. This concern particularly includes an internal attribution of the causes for the mistake, and the individual must consider the locus of control on the situation in the area of his or her competencies.

4. If these first three issues apply, the plausible point of learning from mistakes arises: A reflection upon what has happened and a thorough analysis of the cause must be undertaken in order to help the individual to understand what has happened and what the reasons for the failing were.
5. On this basis, the individual must develop negative knowledge, which is knowledge about how things are not shaped and how things do not work. It is the complementary kind of knowledge about objects and procedures which supplements positive knowledge. Oser refers to several philosophical approaches which claim that real knowledge about objects is not conceivable without negative knowledge (Mayo/Spanos 2010)
6. Finally, individuals have to transfer their knowledge about the mistake to future situations in order to avoid the same mistake in the future.

These steps of learning from mistakes describe general prerequisites. Apparently, learning from mistakes is not facile and it is obvious that it requires different steps of processing an event. Kolodner (1983) came up with a similar model of a dynamic episodic memory, which explains cognitively how an occurrence of mistakes leads from a modification and integration to an updating of knowledge. She explicitly emphasised the importance of reflecting on the mistake in order to analyse and explain its occurrence, and to think about future prevention opportunities. Bauer and Gruber (2007) define learning from mistakes as a special case of experiential learning in terms of an establishment and a modification of scripts and routines. Resumptive learning from mistakes can be described as a detection of a mistake, its dissection, explanation, replacement and the adoption of new knowledge and strategies.

All these approaches of learning from mistakes can be applied to each domain and each empirical field. Oser and Spychiger focus on school contexts, mainly in the interaction between pupils and teachers. Seifried and Baumgartner (2009) focused on those interactions within vocational educational settings (e.g. gastronomy, Baumgartner and Seifried in this volume); Harteis, Bauer, and Gruber (2008) investigated inhouse ways of dealing with mistakes within industrial enterprises. However, all these studies revealed problems and difficulties in the empirical investigation.

There is thus a general theoretical pattern available, which describes steps and prerequisites of learning from mistakes. However, the challenges discussed above reveal difficulties in declaring an incident as a mistake. The challenges relate to issues of social interaction, whereas the theoretical pattern describes steps which have to be cognitively processed by the individual. The fact that there is a lack of empirical foundation of learning from mistakes in business contexts may not be due to the lack of theories but due to the imponderability of social interactions.

2.5 Challenges for Research and Business Practice

By acknowledging the importance of learning from mistakes for educational research as well as for business management and facing the issues discussed in this article, the following goals can be suggested for research and business practice.

2.5.1 Challenges for Research

Besides organising field access and recruiting participants or subjects, the choice of research questions and research methods has to be taken into consideration for future research. In general, the choice of method depends on the choice of research question. It is obvious that results of a behaviouristic point of view show different research approaches and findings compared to a cognitive perspective. Additionally, the choice of macro-, meso-, and micro-perspectives generate different empirical data sets. The choice of, for example, a micro-perspective, like the study on nurses and their learning from errors at work (Bauer 2008), creates important explorative data. Nevertheless, the question arises regarding the extent of the validity of this data set for the macro-perspective. Future research demands approaches which combine macro- and micro-perspectives, because those approaches consider the organisation and the subject with equal importance.

A certain methodological challenge still needs to be solved regarding researching mistakes. It is a basic goal of empirical research to keep information comparable across several subjects. This raises challenges for researching learning from mistakes when the issue of authenticity emerges: Either participants report and reflect on mistake situations which they really experienced, or participants have to reflect on a mistake situation presented by researchers. In the first case, participants have the opportunity to describe factual ways of dealing with mistakes in their work environment. Research can access factual working practices (unless the individual does not report what really happened). However, a pattern needs to be developed to make different authentic experiences in the context of different but comparable working environments in order to find general answers in this research area. In the second case, all participants reflect on the same case, so that their answers can be directly compared. However, participants must describe what they think about their reactions in their work environment. In this case, research can merely access hypothetical work practices. The issue of authenticity is a common problem of researching learning processes. Researchers commonly imply that the participants are aware of the learning process. However, that is not necessarily the case (Bauer/Gruber 2007). The development of comparable experiences strongly demands the researcher's competence in the inhouse processes. The offered experience should be relevant to the individual and/or the organisation. Otherwise, the output is not useful. It is advisable to every enterprise to conduct qualitative research in order to explore the processes and conditions relevant to learning from mistakes. A triangulation study design should be taken into consideration to increase the validity and reliability of the data, especially in this complex area of research. Further research should aim at developing a framework which enables researchers to compare cases of authentic mistake.

Reason (1990) already made an attempt by distinguishing different types of mistakes. He defined two categories of mistakes: on the one hand, slips (the occurrence of attention problems) and lapses (the occurrence of memory failure) and on the other hand, knowledge- and rule-based mistakes. These types reflect different mental activities which lead to a mistake. Mental activities comprise, for example, awareness, deliberate action planning, or risk calculation. Different types of mistakes offer different learning potential and, thus, maybe demand different strategies of learning. The occurrence of a lapse might indicate the need for better memory strategies, whereas a knowledge-based mistake might demand training for the whole company staff.

To distinguish the scope of a mistake's effects might be another opportunity. It is plausible to assume that "small" mistakes, which concern just the failing person, will be handled and reflected on differently than "big" mistakes, which concern many people. Different cases can then be compared according to the scope of their impact. A third option for the investigation of individual learning from mistakes considers emotional feelings related to a mistake – and here psychological constructs like overconfidence (Armor/ Taylor 2002; Gigerenzer 1991; Tversky/Kahneman 1982) or psychological safety and the comfort zone (Edmonson 1999) might be of relevance. Psychology can focus on the experiences and the inner-mental processes of an employee in a faulty situation. This psychological issue points out the requirement of an interdisciplinary and back coupling research between educational and psychological research. The findings of psychological investigations can support and optimise professional action guidelines in an educational content. So far, educational research lacks such a framework, which could help to overcome some of the previously discussed challenges.

2.5.2 Challenges for Business Practice

Recent concepts of business organisation claim permanent change and development and demand employees who are able to successfully cope with customers' and markets' demands. Such a goal cannot be achieved by detailed rules but demands innovation and creativity. As future development is not always precisely foreseeable, enterprises must conduct experiments in order to gain success in the market. Experiments always imply the possibility of failing. Hence, innovative behaviour within an enterprise includes an open mind towards mistakes and the tendency to work on mistakes cooperatively. However, this is not a recent insight, but rather well-recognised in the context of business philosophies.

The crucial issue is that enterprises manage to practically apply business philosophy – in effect, to establish practices of social behaviour that would reflect the ideas of business philosophies. Usually, enterprises put huge effort into organisational development, which aims precisely at realising business philosophy. However, enterprises understandably view these efforts as their own private sphere and are thus seldom open to independent research support. It is a huge challenge for business practice to implement independent field research, which can be conducted either by inhouse departments (e.g. organisational development), consultants, or research institutes. Independent research, of course, implies the possibility of finding out uncomfortable truths, if obvious gaps between programmatic ideas of business philosophies and practices of social behaviour are indicated.

2.6 Conclusion

Learning from mistakes is an issue of high relevance to educational research and business practice. This article has discussed different problems related to the issue of mistakes. The slow but steady progress in publications on learning from mistakes indicates that at least researchers acknowledge the relevance of mistakes for learning purposes. Business organisation has to deal with mistakes from the start. Taylor and Ford therefore established a system of rigid regulations in order to avoid mistakes. More recent approaches of business organisation established flexible structures in order to cope with unforeseeable market developments. Since enterprises usually do not publish results of inhouse developmental efforts, it is unclear how effective business organisations realise business philosophies nowadays in implementing flexible structures, and in identifying what role learning from mistakes plays in the success of these business organisations. There is huge potential for both researchers as well as business organisers to bring together business interests and independent research interests in order to improve business organisation and enhance insight into learning from mistakes in daily working life.

References

Appelbaum, S./Gallagher, J. (2000): The competitive advantage of organizational learning. In: *Journal of Workplace Learning: Employee Counselling Today*, 12, 2, pp. 40-56.

Argyris, C. (1999): *On organizational learning*, 2nd edn., Maldern: Blackwell.

Armor, D.A./Taylor, S.E. (2002): When predictions fail: The dilemma of unrealistic optimism. In: Gilovich, T./Griffin, D./Kahneman, D. (eds.): *Heuristics and biases. The psychology of intuitive judgment*. Cambridge: Cambridge University Press, pp. 334-347

Baer, M.,/Frese, M. (2003): Innovation is not enough: climates for initiative and psychological safety, process inventions, and firm performance. In: *Journal of Organizational Behavior*, 24, pp. 45- 68.

Baud, D./Garrick, J. (1999): *Understanding learning at work*. London: Routledge.

Bauer, J. (2008): *Learning from errors at work. Studies on nurses' engagement in error-related learning activities*. Regensburg: University of Regensburg.

Bauer, J./Gruber, H. (2007): Workplace changes and workplace learning: Advantages of an educational micro perspective. In: *International Journal of Lifelong Education*, 26, pp. 675-688.

Bauer, J./Festner, D./Harteis, C./Heid, H./Gruber, H. (2004): Fehlerorientierung im betrieblichen Alltag. *Zeitschrift für Berufs- und Wirtschaftspädagogik*, 100, pp. 65-82.

Edmonson, A.C. (1999): Psychological safety and working behavior in work teams. *Administrative Science Quarterly*, 44, pp. 350-383.

Enderle, G. (2007): The ethics of conviction versus the ethics of responsibility: A false antithesis for business ethics. In: *Journal of Human Values*, 13(2), pp. 83-94.

Ford, H. (2007/1922): *My life and work*. New York: Cosimo.

Gigerenzer, G. (1991): From tools to theories: A heuristic of discovery in cognitive psychology. In: *Psychological Review*, 98, pp. 254-267.

Glendon, A.I./Clark, S./McKenna, E. F. (2006). *Human safety and risk management*. London: Chapman & Hall.

Graupner, H.-B. (2001). *Karriere: einsteigen, aufsteigen, umsteigen*. Freiburg im Breisgau: Haufe.

Harteis, C./Bauer, J./Gruber, H. (2008): The culture of learning from mistakes: How employees handle mistakes in everyday work. In: *International Journal for Educational Research*, 47, pp. 223–231.

Heid, H. (1991): Problematik einer Erziehung zur Verantwortungsbereitschaft. In: *Neue Sammlung*, 31, pp. 459-481.

Imai, M. (1986): *Kaizen. The key to Japan's competitive success*. New York: McGraw-Hill.

Kolodner, J. (1983): Towards an understanding of the role of experience in the evolution from novice to expert. In: *International Journal of Man-Machine Studies*, 19, pp. 497-518.

Kühl, S. (2000): *Das Regenmacher- Phänomen: Widersprüche und Aberglaube im Konzept der lernenden Organisation*. Frankfurt/Main: Campus Verlag.

Mayo, D.G./Spanos, A. (2010): *Error and inference. Recent exchanges on experimental reasoning, reliability, and the objectivity and rationality of science.* New York: Cambridge University Press.
Oser, F./Hascher, T./Spychiger, M. (1999): Lernen aus Fehlern. Zur Psychologie des negativen Wissens. In W. Althof (Eds.), *Fehlerwelten. Vom Fehlermachen und Lernen aus Fehlern* . Opladen: Leske+Budrich, pp. 11-41.
Oser, F./Spychiger, M. (2005): *Lernen ist schmerzhaft. Zur Theorie des negativen Wissens und zur Praxis der Fehlerkultur.* Weinheim: Beltz.
Putz, D./Schilling, J./Kluge, A. (submitted): Measuring organizational climate to learn from errors. In: Bauer, J./ Harteis, C. (eds.): *Human fallability: The ambiguity of errors for work and learning.* Dordrecht: Springer.
Reason, J. T. (1990): *Human error.* Cambridge: Cambridge University Press.
Rybowiak, V./Garst, H./Frese, M./Batinic, B. (1999): Error orientation questionnaire (EOQ): Reliability, validity, and different language equivalence. *Journal of Organizational Behaviour*, 20, pp. 527- 547.
Seifried, J./Baumgartner, A. (2009): Lernen aus Fehlern in der betrieblichen Ausbildung – Problemfeld und möglicher Forschungszugang. In: *Berufs- und Wirtschaftspädagogik online (bwp@)*, 17. Retrieved April 11, 2011, from http:// www.bwpat.de/ausgabe17/seifried_ baumgartner_bwpat17.pdf.
Senge, P. (1994): *Fifth discipline fieldbook: Strategies for building a learning organization.* New York: Brealey.
Slattery, M. (2003): *Key ideas of sociology.* Cheltenham: Nelson Thornes.
Taylor, F.W. (1939/1911): *The principles of scientific management.* New York: Harper & Row.
Tennant, M. (1999): *Is learning transferable?* In: Baud, D./Garrick, J. (eds.): *Understanding learning at work.* London: Routledge, pp. 165-179.
Tversky, A./Kahneman, D. (1982): Evidential impact of base rates. In: Kahneman, D./ Slovic, P./Tversky, A. (eds.): *Judgment under uncertainty: Heuristics and biases.* Cambridge: Cambridge University Press, pp. 153-160.
van Dyck, C. (2009): Mastering the dual challenges of errors: Risk and uncertainty as contingencies for control and learning. In: *Journal of Applied Occupational Sciences*, 2, pp. 4-13.
van Dyck, C./Frese, M./Baer, M./Sonnentag, S. (2005): Organizational error management culture and its impact on performance: A two-study replication. In: *Journal of Applied Psychology*, 90, pp. 1228- 1240.
Vester, F. (2002): *The art of interconnected thinking: Tools and concepts for a new approach to tackling complexity.* Munich: mcb.
Wuttke, E./Seifried, J./Mindnich, A. (2008): Umgang mit Fehlern und Ungewissheit. In: Gläser-Zikuda, M./Seifried, J. (eds.), *Lehrexpertise – Analyse und Bedeutung unterrichtlichen Handelns.* Münster: Waxmann, pp. 91-111.

3 Learning from Errors – Strategies for Accounting Lessons – Outline of a Research Project

Maxi Link

3.1 The Need for a Cognitive Perspective on Learning from Errors

For many years now, scientists from different research fields – especially the educational sector – have concentrated their research on errors and their function in learning processes (Althof 1999; Yerushalmi/Polingher 2006). Although the first half of the 20th century was mostly influenced by the view that errors, as disagreeable divergences, had to be avoided during learning processes (Weimer 1930), nowadays they are mostly seen as important and precious steps within human development (Oser/Spychiger 2005; Cannon/Edmondson 2005). This crucial change of argumentation was achieved through a constructivist perspective, arguing that errors (in terms of perturbations) are essential initiators for learning and reflection processes, since they dispose the individual to reorganize its cognitive structures (Minnameier 2008).

In light of these facts, it is obvious that the concept of learning from errors can be understood as an essential didactical and methodological concept for teaching and learning processes (ibid.). In the meantime, a new discussion about the 'correct' handling of errors has emerged for both the scholarly and the professional field of learning (Ginat 2003; Tjosvold/Yu/Hui 2004). However, most of these concepts primarily focus on motivational and emotional aspects of error (management) culture or "error friendliness" (Spychiger 2003; van Dyck/Frese/Baer/Sonnentag 2005). They do not take instructionally relevant aspects of a more cognitive view of learning processes into account. For that reason, (educational) science is still not able either to define the cognitive causes of erroneous thoughts precisely, categorize these processes to specific types of errors or define strategies related to the occurring errors in order to help students learn from them.

A promising entry point to a comprehensive explication of types and causes of errors in thinking processes may be given by the inferential theory of scientific inquiry. This theory allows the analysis and instructional intervention of learning processes. Its main features and applications will be discussed in the following paragraph.

3.2 The Inferential Access: Identifying, Classifying and Dealing with Errors

The inferential theory of learning is based on the epistemic approach of Charles S. Peirce (1898/1992; 1903/1997) and has been advanced by Minnameier (2004, 2005; in press; in this volume). This approach conceptualizes the process of knowledge acquisition as *logical processes* in the broader sense. Taking that into account, logic is not only defined as deductive reasoning, but also as abductive and inductive processes. The interrelation of these processes can be visualized in the *inferential triad*, which offers a complete account of the whole process of inquiry (Minnameier 2004: 76). According to this theory and a (moderate) constructivist view of learning, new knowledge is inferred from prior knowledge. The three inferences can be characterized in the following way (Minnameier 2005: 95ff.; Figure 1 shows the dynamic relationship):

1. *Abduction* describes a creative inference from a new (personal) problem or fact which has to be explained to possible solutions or plausible explanations. The only criterion of validity for abductive inferences is the solution or elimination of the original problem.
1. *Deduction* denotes the inference from what is assumed to consequences that necessarily result from the premise. The necessity that the consequences have to be a result of the premise is also the criterion of validity for deductive inferences.[1]
2. *Induction* denotes the inference from empirical observations to the decision of whether a theory can be approved or must be refused. Thus, the theoretical assertions are generalized to all cases of the reference framework (past, present and future ones). An inductive inference is only valid if all other possible explanations can be excluded (seen from the cognitive perspective of the epistemic subject).

Figure 1: The dynamic interrelation of the three inferences

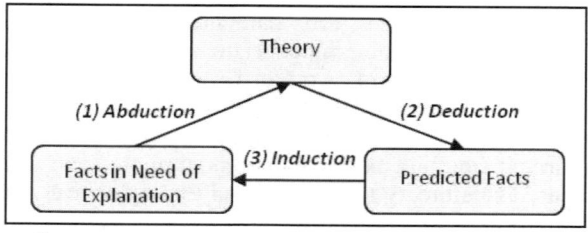

Source: own diagram

---

[1] Empirical assertions mostly result from the deductive method of scientific inquiry.

Furthermore, each of the three inferences consists of three sub-steps, namely colligation, observation and judgment (Peirce 1898/1992; 1903/1997).

1. *Colligation:* This inferential step refers to the collection of the (case-specific) relevant premises.
2. *Observation:* In a second step, these premises will be observed, in order to generate a result which is specific for the current inference. However, the result is generated spontaneously, meaning that the validity of the result will not be proven in this step.
3. *Judgment:* Eventually, the judgment constitutes the inference of retrospective examination and judgment of the result referred to the current criterion of validity (depending on the type of the current inference).

As a consequence of this three/three separation, it is possible to distinguish nine correlations, which can be used as analytical tools for thinking processes. Since errors can occur within all these differentiations, this scheme offers a possibility to localize as well as typify errors in logical reasoning (see Table 1).

Table 1: Matrix of error types in logical reasoning

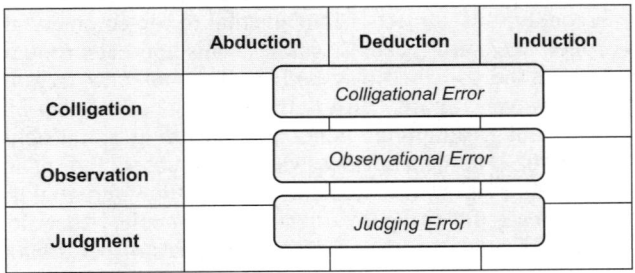

Source: own table

Agreeing with Wehner and Mehl (2010), who emphasize that "erroneous behavior follows logical principles, even though it's not always easy to recognize" (p. 17, translated by ML), this matrix allows the pursuit of correct and erroneous learning processes as well as the methods through which students understand and implement instructions of the teacher.[2] Instructions which are able to facilitate the detection and correction of errors that *actually occur* can be derived from a *preceding* inferential analysis of the intended learning processes. Therefore, the inferential analysis (of errors) can take two different perspectives (see Table 2):

---

2   Instructional advices also can be given by group members or peers.

Table 2: Prospective and retrospective perspectives of the inferential analysis

Prospective Dimension	Retrospective Dimension	Insight into…
Anticipation of the intended processes of knowledge acquisition and its application.	Analysis of actually performed processes of knowledge acquisition and its application.	The "logic" of errors.
Anticipation of errors that could occur.	Analysis of errors that actually occur.	
Anticipation of specific instructional strategies that might facilitate learning from the error.	Analysis of the actual process of learning from errors.	The "mechanism" of error-based learning and teaching.

Source: own table

It can be noticed that there is a specific didactic added value of this differentiation as it allows us to focus the general process of learning and error-related instructions on the ideal path of logical reasoning (see Figure 1).

Link and Minnameier (2008)/Minnameier and Link (2010) elaborated this approach towards the subject-specific didactics of accounting in school. This benchmark was chosen because accounting is essential, due to two main reasons. Firstly, it plays a key role in understanding economic issues and processes. Secondly, this subject is fundamental to the commercial sector as well as to economics and/or business studies. This approach roughly follows the basic ideas of the so-called *wirtschaftsinstrumentelles Rechnungswesen* (Preiß 1999). However, it partly differs from the didactical path insofar as it consists of different assumptions concerning learning and teaching (Minnameier/Link 2010). The general idea was to restructure the didactical path as well as the level of tasks, which belong to the entire inferential triad.[3]

For this purpose, the structure of the chosen subject-specific didactics was partly changed, and cognitive conflicts (in terms of perturbations) were embodied to fulfill a (moderate) constructivist view of learning (see Figure 2). Each unit, which is subdivided into particular learning tasks, was then inferentially analyzed regarding the required thinking/learning processes. With regard to the inferential analysis, it was possible to anticipate which kinds of errors may occur while dealing with a task or problem. An instructional manual was thus elaborated, explaining how to deal with each single error in its inferential category.

---

[3] It is therefore emphasized that not only deductive but also inductive and abductive processes are essential to solve a task or problem.

Figure 2: Partial modeling of the contextual structure for an introduction into accounting

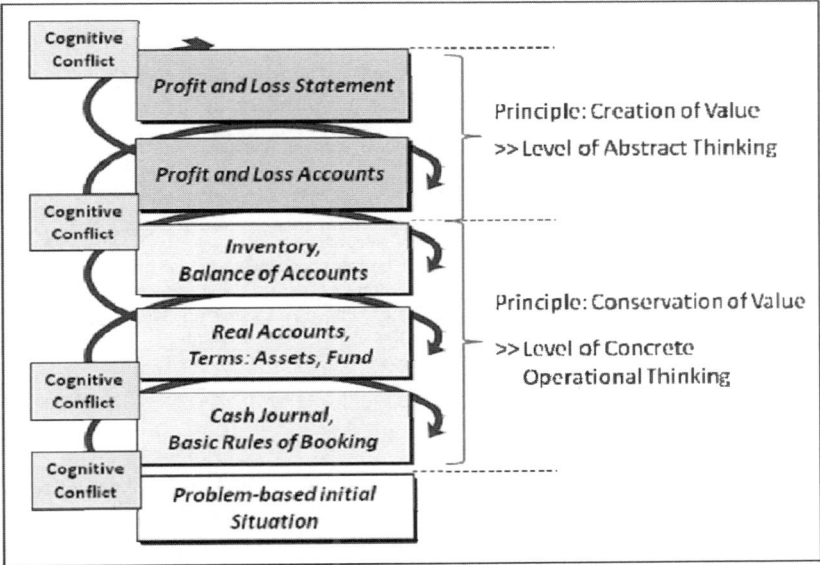

Source: adapted from Minnameier/Link 2010

The above outlined sequence of analytic steps, which allows us to derive error specific instructions, will be illustrated in Table 3, using the example of the problem-based initial situation of the didactical path (see Figure 2). The abductive inference of the solution process will be focused exemplarily.

Table 3: Exemplary sequence of the derivation of error specific instructions

Problem-based initial Situation and Task	
A young apprentice lost track of her financial situation and cannot understand why she is nearly bankrupt for this month. Task: to find a strategy to (1) have her budget under control and (2) to calculate her current budget	
Inferential Reconstruction of the Approach	
Inductive Conclusion	Problem: Budget not under control: Need for action!
Abduction to an adequate Strategy	Strategy: To list all earnings and expenses and to balance them.
Deductive Application of the Strategy	Listing of all earnings and expenses of the month.
Inductive Verification of the Strategy	Problem is solved appropriately and the strategy is sustainable.

Table 3: Exemplary sequence of the derivation of error specific instructions (cont.)

Anticipation of possibly occurring Errors in Abduction	
Colligational Error	One does not regard that a stable strategy is demanded (premise), or: One does not understand the problem and does not use prior knowledge to interpret the situation.
Observational Error	One does not find a strategy, or: One abduces a false strategy. Example: "Just do not squander money."
Judging Error	One does not check one's strategy for plausibility, or: One accepts the (false) strategy with unsuitable reasons.
Anticipation of error-related Instructions to facilitate Abduction	
Instruction to Colligate	Recapitulate the problem described here and possible reasons of it! Use your own experience in dealing with money!
Instruction to Observe	Could it be helpful to take a look at the structure and the information content of the current accounts?
Instruction to Judge	Check the usefulness of your strategy regarding the problem described here!

Source: own table

Therefore, the question arises as to how possible it may be to successfully implement this concept and instructional advices into accounting lessons. In order to be able to answer this question, the following subquestions have to be analyzed:

– To what extent do the participants actually acquire their knowledge along an ideal path of learning and teaching?
– To what extent do the participants make mistakes and which kinds of errors occur? and:
– To what extent are error-related advices and instructions successful and how effectively do these strategies facilitate learning from errors?

The following chapter presents a methodological approach that seems suitable for testing these kinds of issues, which are outlined above.

3.3 Methodological Approach: The Instructional Support and Analysis of Learning from Errors

3.3.1 Methodological Framework: A Microgenetic Study with Design-Based Research Elements

In order to understand the preceding procedures behind the visible results of learning processes, *the microgenetic method* could be a suitable research design (Siegler/Crowley 1991; Siegler 1995). Microgenetic studies try to visualize the characteristics of conceptual change, i.e., acquiring specific data about cognitive development. For that purpose, individuals are observed throughout the entire period of change, which is characterized by a high density of observations as well as a closer look at the occurring qualitative and quantitative changes (Siegler/Crowley 1991: 606).

This method is a capable one, due to the fact that the tested sample is supposed to produce basic knowledge of fundamental commercial principles within a short period of time. The involved (developmental) processes can only be captured by constant and exact observations. Pre-/Post-Designs, which only show the level of knowledge before and after a pedagogical intervention, are not suitable: they neither allow the effect of a didactical design to be captured nor the constituting steps of knowledge acquisition to be reconstructed (Siegler 1995: 226). Meanwhile, the microgenetic method allows us to gain a basic insight into changes in thinking and knowledge acquisition. Moreover, the reasons for change can be established, and conclusions on the prognostic quality and instructional functionality of the didactical design can thus be drawn. For these reasons, the microgenetic method is suitable for comprehending and inferentially analyzing learning progresses.

In order to acquire reliable information about the practicability and functionality of the instructional design, a certain amount of test runs must be carried out. This study will consist of a *sequence of three separate runs*. This amount seems to be sufficient for a first empirical access point, since a vast amount of data output can be expected for each run. The gained experiences of each test run will be integrated into the next, in order to see didactical improvements (Collins, Joseph and Bielaczyc [2004: 18] call this the approach of progressive refinement). The test runs of this study will therefore cyclically pass steps of *test*, *validation* and *gradual redesign* (see Figure 3).

Consequently, the didactical design of the instructional approach will also be highlighted in this study (besides the inferential design of the units and the learning tasks). With regard to this, the study is also characterized by *attributes of design-based research* (Brown 1992; Cobb/Confrey/diSessa/Lehrer/Schauble 2003).

Each of the three test runs will be evaluated separately and thus will give information as to whether or not the instructional design must be modified. Therefore, the functionality of instruction design can be determined by reconstructing the progress of students' learning: if the didactical and instructional design is functionally efficient, the reconstruction shows that correct thinking and thus successfully initiated learning from errors is set out.

Figure 3: Cyclical improvement of the instructional design in terms of a design experiment

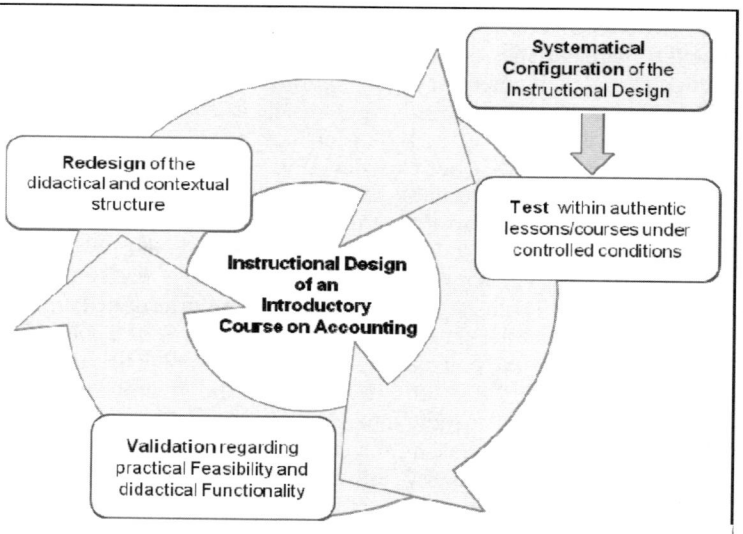

Source: own diagram

Design-based research is basically used to design and to test interventions that include specific theories of learning, thinking and teaching. Moreover, it always (re)presents a particular understanding of the interdependency of theory, designed artifacts, and practice (The Design-Based Research Collective, 2003: 6).[4] Regarding the subject of this study, the underlying theory of learning and thinking is the inferential rationale (see Chapter 2), which is extended to learning from errors in logical reasoning. Therefore, the already above-mentioned interdependency includes the following elements: (1) a prospective analysis of a person's train of thought and its included errors, (2)

---

4 With regard to this case, Collins et al (2004, p. 19) stress that design-based research is not only a refining practice, but that an effective design research will also address the theoretical questions and issues of the topic.

the corresponding didactical path and instructional strategies to stimulate learning from errors and (3) a retrospective analysis of the pedagogical scenario to evaluate the effectiveness as well as efficiency of that arrangement.

In order to conduct this specific type of qualitative research, *one-on-one-tutorials* seem to be a promising method. It can be helpful to create a small-scale version of a learning ecology, which can be analyzed in depth and detail (Cobb et al. 2003: 9). In this case the researcher, who is also the teacher (later called 'teacher-experimenter'), holds several teaching lessons to one proband at a time. The next chapter illustrates the methodological conception of these tutorials, which is necessary for a meaningful data collection on the learning environment and the students' reasoning.

3.3.2 Data Collection: The Think Aloud Method

Since cognitive processes cannot be directly observed (Hussy/Schreier/ Echterhoff 2010), methodological "tricks" of research are necessary to achieve the desired outcome. The *Think Aloud Method* is one example to trigger processes which can help to acquire final results (van Someren et al. 1994; Kucan/Beck 1997; Konrad 2010).[5] Supported by a direct and intensive mode of interaction during the tutorials, the sample will be stimulated to think loudly: the students are asked to verbalize their thinking processes (e.g. their ideas and strategies as well as the problems or irritations that occur). Therefore, this method combines two opportunities of acquiring data – the collection of verbal data with the stimulation of introspection (Hussy et al. 2010: 226).[6] This qualitative research process is often used in cognitive theoretical error analysis and was already applied during a preliminary study of Link and Minnameier (2008) successfully. Other authors such as Hasemann (1985) have included this approach in recent studies of students' errors. These two facts only intensify the need to reiterate this method in the current study. Contrary to the common practice (Cotton/Gresty 2006; Hussy et al. 2010), specific questions of the teacher-experimenter are allowed here, since they are able to stimulate the learner's introspection and verbalization of his or her thoughts.[7]

---

5   Kucan and Beck (1997: 272) emphasize the necessity of such a method, but they also argue that the growing number of studies using this approach maintains its validity.
6   According to Konrad (2010) there are three different types of thinking loudly: *introspection* (immediate verbalization), *immediate retrospection* (occurring immediately after the introspection) and *delayed retrospection* (occurring immediately after completing a task).
7   The teacher-experimenter, in a way, takes the role of a team member asking his/her partner for help or an explanation. For example: By asking for a strategy to solve the described problem the teacher-experimenter can stimulate the participant to verbalize his/her abductive reasoning.

The Think Aloud Method is mostly combined with a recording of the (learning) sessions in order to retain the thoughts of the probands, namely by video camera and/or audio equipment (Cotton/Gresty 2006; Link/Minnameier 2008). Thus, every single (video)sequence can be transcribed and then be inferentially analyzed in detail. Former studies of this subject have shown that video analysis is a reliable method in analyzing errors as well as their treatment[8] (Meyer/Seidel/Prenzel 2006). Therefore, it is planned to stimulate the students' verbalization of thoughts and their verbal interactions with the teacher-experimenter throughout all the lessons.[9] The technical options for the analysis of the data, which will be collected by the help of the Think Aloud Method, are outlined in the following section.

3.3.3 Data Analysis: The Application of an Inferential Code Plan

The data set will be completely transcribed and subsequently analyzed with the help of MAXQDA, which is a software tool for qualitative data analysis. For this, a code plan was developed, which is based on the inferential systematization of thinking processes (see Table 4). This code plan was already successfully applied during the preliminary study of this research project (see Link and Minnameier 2008). The taxonomy of the coding system is able to reduce the problem of high inference measures, which commonly exists in video-based data collection (e.g. Hugener/Pauli/Reusser 2006: 46f.)

Table 4: Extract of the code plan basing of the inferential system of error analysis

Steps of Encoding		Content of Encoding
1st step	Inferential Process	Did the error occur within the abductive, deductive or inductive part of the thinking process?
2nd step	Inferential Subprocess	Did the error occur within the colligation, observation or the judgment?
3rd step	Execution of the Inferential Processes	Subprocess: Was the thinking process correctly, incorrectly or not executed?
		Activity: Was the thinking process proactively executed or retroactively reproduced?
		Correction of the Error: Was the error corrected?
		Reaction to the Correction: Was the correction of the error accepted or was it rejected?

Source: own table

---

8   This is mostly highlighted in the context of error culture.
9   Regarding the plentitude of data that (can) result from video recording, Collins et al (2004: 19) point to the risk of an information overflow. Consequently they stress that data reduction as well as a focused analysis of the data set is needed.

The clear inferential assignment of both the particular steps of the learners and the instructions of the teacher-experimenter leaves just little scope for interpretation in the coding process. Therefore, the interaction of learner and teacher-experimenter can be reconstructed fairly precisely.

Previous research shows that the different types of errors and the processes of their correction can be empirically distinguished (according to the 1st and 2nd step in Table 4) and give information on the performance level of the students (Link/Minnameier 2008).[10]

Despite the strength of this low inference measure, further formal requirements for the performance and analysis of experimental studies have to be considered. These are the *internal (and external) validity* of the microgenetic experiment as well as the *inter-coder reliability* of the data coding (e.g. Huberman/Miles 2002). Moreover *the project results* of this qualitative study must also be validated. The measures which were chosen to meet these requirements are presented in the next chapter.

3.3.4 Validity Criteria of the Methodological Approach

Even though this microgenetic study will be conducted as one-group-experiments, it meets the basic criteria to guarantee *internal validity*. In order to generate a causal relationship between the learning progress of the tested sample and the specific design of the used theory, the experiments will be conducted under strictly controlled conditions. Potentially problematic factors, which will be controlled, are mentioned in the following:

- *The prior knowledge of the participants:* To get a reliable outcome of the research, the instructional design will be tested by students, who are in the eighth grade of general-educational schools.[11] It can be assumed that this target group is not yet familiar with economic issues. Therefore, the course can actually be seen as a first-time introduction into accounting.
- *The intelligence of the participants:* The intelligence of the involved probands might be another influencing factor and therefore will be tested before selecting the sample of the study.[12] Based on the test results, the group will be arranged in such a way that it consists of students with dif-

---

10 The results showed that the rates of abductive and deductive errors of the recorded students nearly balanced each other. Regarding the inferential subprocesses it was discovered that more observational and judging errors than colligational errors occurred. This could be a tentative indication of the relevance of genuine problems of understanding (abduction), miscalculations (deduction) and missing (or erroneous) transformation of colligated premises into adequate approaches in accounting lessons (Minnameier/Link 2008). Results of studies about typical errors in accounting confirm this assumption (Wuttke/Seifried 2010).
11 This corresponds to the ‚Sekundarstufe 1 im Allgemeinbildenden Schulwesen' of the German school system.
12 The intelligence test according to Heller & Perleth (2000) will be used.

fering levels of intelligence.
- *External effects that are relevant for the participants' learning process:* The planned tutorials will be carried out within a neutral learning environment (i.e., not at school). All participants will be taught by one teacher, who uses just one (didactical) method. Such a procedure can avoid personal and/or methodological biases.
- *The emotions and motivation of the participants:* In the sense of a positive error culture the teacher-experimenter will emphasize to the probands that there is no shame in making mistakes and in pointing out comprehension problems. Moreover the learning material and tasks are directed to keep the motivation of the learners going: They will become part of a realistic story and will go along with a central character on her way through the basics of accounting.
- *Deviations from the intended structure of the course:* The learning materials and the teaching strategies are fully elaborated (including all relevant "detours" in learning and error-based instructional strategies). Therefore, the consistence of the instructions is also given for the error-specific interventions of the teacher.

Furthermore it has to be taken into consideration that *the steady demand for thinking aloud might be a secondary treatment.* Though studies have shown that producing verbal reports interferes with quantity aspects ("slow down effect"), it does not cause changes in the quality of thinking processes or solutions (Ericsson/Simon 1980; Deffner 1984). Regarding the study's interest in errors in reasoning, which are primarily qualitative aspects of cognitive processes, this finding endorses the choice of this research design. Some deficits of the think aloud method[13] which must, however, be regarded, can perhaps be compensated by triangulation of the method with retrospection of the probands afterwards (Würffel 2001).

It is not necessary to define further controlling measures with regard to internal validity since the efficiency of the treatment can be observed directly, instead of merely deriving it from the gained results. If the learning processes of the participants occur in the assumed way, not only internal but also *external validity* of the experimental setting is given. In other words, its general validity and independence from any other kind of influences of the learning environment can be claimed, if the effectiveness of the error-based instructions can be approved.

In addition to the internal and external validity of experiments, the *intercoder reliability* of the data coding also influences the quality criteria of qualitative research (Mayring 2004). One appropriate way to guarantee this is to involve several independent coders and to calculate the inter-coder relia-

---

13 Those compensable deficits are, for example, incompleteness of verbalizations and difficulties to interpret paragraphs of transcripts (Würffel 2001).

bility of the outcoming results (using MAXQDA). Regarding the *validation of the project results,* it is intended to use the following instruments (according to Lamnek 2005: 155f):

- Carrying out multiple test runs of the didactical design.
- Comparing notes with other members of the scientific community (who are not involved in the study but are experts in the field of the theoretical position of learning, on which this study is based).
- Paying attention to the adequacy of the data interpretation (which is guaranteed by the theoretical logic of the inferential rationale).
- Verifying the reliance of the research (it is intended to document the implementation of the learning setting as well as the coding and analysis of the thinking processes and the errors in reasoning. Consequently, the entire process of research is comprehensive) and:
- Validating the outcomes of the project, based on a comparison with results of other studies.[14]

Despite the spectrum of instruments listed above, there are potentially problematic factors within the research design that have to be taken into consideration. Finally, the following steps of the research project are outlined below, which also include aspects of their time schedule and working plan.

3.4 Prospects to Realizing the Research Project

As previously mentioned (see Chapter 3.1), three test runs are planned in order to get reliable results concerning the functionality of the instructional approach. These test runs will constitute the *main study* of the research project, commencing in autumn 2011. Each test run will consist of a sample of ten participants as well as ten learning units over a period of ten weeks (one 90-minute tutorial will be held per test person and per week). In the run-up to the main study a *preliminary study* will be conducted in spring 2011 to test the feasibility of the intended methodology and the original time schedule[15]. This preliminary study is also supposed to give information about the impact of the technical components used within the test runs. To minimize possible diversions, the teacher-experimenter will use the first test runs to routinize and optimize the handling of the video camera and/or the audio equipment.

---

14 Those results can be found, for example, in Seifried 2004.
15 It depends on the individual pace of the learners as to how many issues can be covered within the tutorials. Therefore, it may be necessary to make several adjustments regarding the amount of the units.

With regard to the modus of the test runs, it can be assumed that one-on-one-tutorials are more effective than holding classes with 25 or more students (but that is normally the standard working procedure at schools, and thus the practical test for the instructional design). As a result, it would make sense to compare these two kinds of learning environments, taking the efficiency of the instructional design into account. This could be conducted within a (quasi-)experimental *follow-up study,* after the internal validity of this approach will have been assured.

Finally it can be summed up that this research project can offer two main contributions: Primarily, it may contribute to understanding error in logical reasoning as well as to helping students learn from them. Secondarily, this didactical approach may also stimulate the current discussion about contemporary subject-specific didactics of accounting.

References

Althof, W. (ed.) (1999): *Fehlerwelten. Vom Fehlermachen und Lernen aus Fehlern. Beiträge und Nachträge zu einem interdisziplinären Symposium aus Anlaß des 60. Geburtstags von Fritz Oser.* Opladen: Leske+Budrich.

Brown, A.L. (1992): Design experiments: Theoretical and methodological challenges in creating complex interventions in classroom settings. In: *The Journal of the Learning Sciences*, 2, 2, pp. 141-178.

Cannon, M.D./Edmondson, A.C. (2005): Failing to learn and learning to fail (intelligently): How great organizations put failure to work to improve and innovate. In: *Long Range Planning: International Journal of Strategic Management*, 38, 3, pp. 299-319.

Cobb, P./Confrey, J./diSessa, A./Lehrer, R./Schauble, L. (2003): Design experiments in educational research. In: *Educational Researcher*, 32 (1), pp. 9-13.

Collins, A./Joseph, D./Bielaczyc, K.(2004): Design research: Theoretical and methodological issues. In: *The Journal of the Learning Sciences*, 13, 1, pp. 15-42.

Cotton, D./Gresty, K. (2006): Reflecting on the think-aloud method for evaluating e-learning. In: *British Journal of Educational Technology*, 37 (1), pp. 45-54.

Deffner, G. (1984): *Lautes Denken – Untersuchung zur Qualität eines Datenerhebungsverfahrens.* Frankfurt am Main et al.: Lang.

Ericsson, K.A./Simon, H.A. (1993): *Protocol analysis; Verbal reports as data*, revised edn., Cambridge, MA: Bradford books/MIT Press.

Gartmeier, M./Bauer, J./Gruber, H./Heid, H. (2008): Negative knowledge: Understanding professional learning and expertise. In: *Vocations and Learning* (1), pp. 87-103.

Ginat, D. (2003): The greedy trap and learning from mistakes. In: *ACM SIGCSE Bulletin,* 35, 1, pp. 11-15.

Hasemann, K. (1985): Die Beschreibung von Schülerfehlern mit kognitionstheoretischen Modellen. In: *Der Mathematikunterricht – Beiträge zu seiner fach-*

lichen, didaktischen und methodischen Gestaltung. Thementeil: Fehleranalysen – Mathematische Denkprozesse, 31, 6, pp. 6-17.

Heller, K.A./Perleth, C. (2000): *Kognitiver Fähigkeitstest für 4. bis 12. Klassen, Revision: KFT 4-12+R.* Göttingen: Beltz Test.

Huberman, A.M./Miles, M.B. (eds.) (2002): *The qualitative researcher's companion.* Thousand Oaks. CA: Sage Publ.

Hugener, I./Pauli, C./Reusser, K. (2006): Videoanalysen. In: Klieme, E./Pauli, C./Reusser, K. (eds.): Dokumentation der Erhebungs- und Auswertungsinstrumente zur schweizerisch-deutschen Videostudie „Unterrichtsqualität, Lernverhalten und mathematisches Verständnis". *Materialien zur Bildungsforschung, Band 15.* Frankfurt am Main: GFPF.

Hussy, W./Schreier, M./Echterhoff, G. (2010): *Forschungsmethoden in Psychologie und Sozialwissenschaften – für Bachelor.* Berlin [u.a.]: Springer.

Konrad, K. (2010): Lautes Denken. In: Mey, G./Mruck, K. (eds.): *Handbuch Qualitative Forschung in der Psychologie.* Wiesbaden: VS Verlag für Sozialwissenschaften, pp. 476-490.

Kucan, L./Beck, I. (1997): Thinking aloud and reading comprehension research: Inquiry, instruction, and social interaction. In: *Review of Educational Research*, 67, 3, pp. 271-299.

Lamnek, S. (2005): *Qualitative Sozialforschung: Lehrbuch.* 4. Aufl., Basel: Beltz.

Link, M./Minnameier, G. (2008): Dem Fehler auf der Spur – Videobasierte Analyse von Denkprozessen und -fehlern im kaufmännischen Unterricht. In: Münk, D./Breuer, K./Deißinger, T. (eds.): *Berufs- und Wirtschaftspädagogik – Probleme und Perspektiven aus nationaler und internationaler Sicht.* Opladen/Farmington Hills: Budrich, pp. 134-143.

Mayring, P. (2004): Qualitative content analysis. In Flick, U./von Kardorf, E./Steinke, I. (eds.): *A companion to qualitative research.* London: Sage, pp. 266 – 269.

Meyer, L./Seidel, T./Prenzel, M. (2006): Wenn Lernsituationen zu Leistungssituationen werden: Untersuchung zur Fehlerkultur in einer Videostudie. In: *Revue suisse des sciences de l'éducation*, 28 ,1, pp. 21-41.

Minnameier, G. (2004): Peirce-suit of truth – why inference to the best explanation and abduction ought not to be confused. In: *Erkenntnis*, 60, pp. 75-105.

Minnameier, G. (2005): *Wissen und inferentielles Denken: Zur Analyse und Gestaltung von Lehr-Lern-Prozessen.* Wien et al: Lang.

Minnameier, G. (2008): Zur empirischen Analyse des Umgangs mit Fehlern im wirtschaftskundlichen Unterricht. In: Münk, D./Gonon, P./Breuer, K./Deißinger, T. (eds.): *Modernisierung der Berufsbildung – Neue Forschungserträge und Perspektiven der Berufs- und Wirtschafspädagogik.* Opladen: Budrich, pp. 120-130.

Minnameier, G./Link, M. (2010): Jenseits des wirtschaftsinstrumentellen Rechnungswesens – ein kognitiv-struktureller und inferentieller Ansatz. In: Seifried, J./Wuttke, E./Nickolaus, R./Sloane, P.F.E. (eds.): *Lehr-Lernforschung in der kaufmännischen Berufsbildung – Ergebnisse und Gestaltungsaufgaben. Beiheft 23 der Zeitschrift für Berufs- und Wirtschaftspädagogik.* Stuttgart: Franz Steiner Verlag, pp. 107-121.

Minnameier, G. (in press): The logicality of abduction, deduction and induction. In: Bergman, M./Paavola, S./Pietarinen, A.V./Rydenfelt, H. (eds.): *Ideas in action:*

Procedures of the applying Peirce conference. Helsinki: Nordic Pragmatism Network.
Oser, F./Spychiger, M. (2005): *Lernen ist schmerzhaft: Zur Theorie des Negativen Wissens und zur Praxis der Fehlerkultur.* Basel: Beltz.
Peirce, C.S. (1898/1992): *Reasoning and the logic of things. The Cambridge conferences lectures of 1898* (ed. by Kenneth Laine Ketner). Cambridge, Mass.: Harvard University Press.
Peirce, C.S. (1903/1997): *Pragmatism as a principle and method of right thinking: The 1903 Harvard lectures on pragmatism* (ed. by Patricia A. Turrisi). Albany: State University of New York Press.
Preiß, P. (1999): *Didaktik des wirtschaftsinstrumentellen Rechnungswesens.* Wien: Oldenbourg.
Seifried, J. (2004): *Fachdidaktische Variationen in einer selbstorganisationsoffenen Lernumgebung: Eine empirische Untersuchung des Rechnungswesenunterrichts.* Wiesbaden: Deutscher Universitätsverlag.
Siegler, R./Crowley, K. (1991): The microgenetic method: A direct means for studying cognitive development. In: *American Psychologist*, 46 ,6, pp. 602-620.
Siegler, R. (1995): How does change occur: A microgenetic study of number conservation. In: *Cognitive Psychology*, 25, pp. 225-273.
Spychiger, M. (2003): Fehler als Fenster auf den Lernprozess. Zur Entwicklung einer Fehlerkultur in der Praxisausbildung. In: *Journal für LehrerInnenausbildung*, 2, pp. 31-38.
The Design-Based Research Collective (2003): Design-based research: An emerging paradigm for educational inquiry. In: *Educational Researcher*, 32, 1, pp. 5-8.
Tjosvold, D./Yu, Z.Y./Hui, C. (2004): Team Learning from Mistakes: The Contribution of Cooperative Goals and Problem-Solving. In: *Journal of Management Studies*, 41, 7, pp. 1223-1245.
Yerushalmi, E./Polingher, C. (2006): Guiding students to learn from mistakes. In: *Physics Education*, 41, 6, pp. 532-537.
van Dyck, C./Frese, M./Baer, M./Sonnentag, S. (2005): Organizational error management culture and its impact on performance: a two-study replication. In: *Journal of Applied Psychology*, 90, 6, pp. 1228-1240.
van Someren, M./Barnard, Y./Sandberg, J. (1994): *The think aloud method: A practical guide to modeling cognitive processes.* London: Academic.
Wehner, T./Mehl, K. (2010): Welche Lerngelegenheiten bieten Fehler? In: *ILS Mail*, 10 (2), pp. 17.
Weimer, H. (1930): Fehlerbekämpfung. In: Nohl, H./Pallat, L. (eds.): *Handbuch der Pädagogik, Band III: Allgemeine Didaktik und Erziehungslehre.* Langensalza: Beltz, pp. 119-128.
Würffel, N. (2001): Protokolle Lauten Denkens als Grundlage für die Erforschung von hypertextgeleiteten Lernprozessen im Fremdsprachenunterricht. In: Müller-Hartmann, A./Schocker-von Dietfurth, M. (eds.): *Qualitative Forschung im Bereich Fremdsprachen lehren und lernen.* Tübingen: Narr, pp. 163-186.
Wuttke, E./Seifried, J. (2010): Students' errors: how teachers diagnose them and how they respond to them. In: *Empirical Research in Vocational Education and Training*, 2, 2, pp. 147-162.

4 The Student Perspective on Dealing with Errors in Mathematics Class[1]

Aiso Heinze, Stefan Ufer, Stefanie Rach and Kristina Reiss

4.1 Introduction

"Mistakes are often the best teachers." "Aus Fehlern wird man klug." "Erreur n'est pas crime." In many languages all over the world, we find proverbs about errors. Interestingly, many of these proverbs attribute a positive function to errors. This indicates the existence of a cumulative human experience in which errors can have positive effects. Most human beings, however, associate negative feelings with errors, which probably stems from the fact that errors are one of the most important criteria in evaluating the performance of individual actions.

In this article, we consider the role of errors during the learning process in a mathematics class. Based on a theoretical framework and results of previous empirical studies, we present findings from a survey on students' perception of error-handling when learning mathematics in school. We want to stress that our perspective on errors differs from the specific diagnostic research perspective of other studies in mathematics education research. Our goal is not to analyze why a learner makes an error and which individual misconceptions or problems are responsible for this. Instead, we focus on the error-handling activities that teachers and students employ in mathematics lessons. The main questions asked are how students experience the activities of their teachers in error situations and how students individually use their own errors as learning opportunities.

4.2 Theoretical Background

The notions "error" or "mistake" are used in various situations and with various meanings in everyday language. In approaching the concept "error" from a scientific perspective, giving a precise definition is challenging. Oser and Spychiger (2005) define an error as a process or a fact that does not

---

[1] This research was funded by the Deutsche Forschungsgemeinschaft (DFG), grant number RE 1247/4 and by the Federal State Hamburg (research program "komdif – Kompetenzmodelle als Basis für eine diagnosegestützte individuelle Förderung").

match a given norm. Based on the theory of negative knowledge, they postulate that the explanation and understanding of errors or incorrect facts and processes are necessary for individuals to distinguish between correct processes or facts (with respect to the norm) and the incorrect surroundings. It should be noted that errors in this sense refer to results of individual learning or problem-solving processes, as opposed to residual error variances of a larger sample such as is usually treated in statistical modeling. Moreover, some researchers divide errors into subcategories (e.g. Bauer/Mulder 2007). For example, Reason (1995) distinguishes simple execution failures for highly structured (e.g. algorithmic) tasks (slips or lapses) on the one hand, and failures in planning or problem solving situations caused by conceptual misunderstandings (mistakes) on the other hand. Since our research is concerned with the general use of errors as a learning opportunity, and since algorithmic failures may also uncover gaps in conceptual understanding, we subsume both types under the term "error" here.

In Section 4.2.1, we give a short overview about the theory of negative knowledge and discuss cognitive and affective aspects of learning processes through error experiences. In Section 4.2.2 we summarize empirical findings concerning error-handling activities in the context of mathematics class from different perspectives. The lack of an existing empirical basis was the initial point of interest for the study presented in this contribution.

4.2.1 Theory of Negative Knowledge and the Role of Errors

The theory of negative knowledge postulates that individuals accumulate two complementary types of knowledge: positive knowledge about correct facts and procedures and negative knowledge about incorrect facts and procedures (e.g. Minsky 1994). Negative knowledge is considered as an essential component of knowledge, since it allows for the identification of boundaries of correct facts and procedures and therefore the ability to distinguish between correct and incorrect facts and procedures. Error-making is related to the negative knowledge of an individual in two ways. On the one hand, negative knowledge has a control function on a meta-level. Since an individual knows about incorrect facts and processes, she/he can reduce the probability of making errors in areas associated with this negative knowledge. On the other hand, errors play an important role for the acquisition of negative knowledge. Since individuals are not usually taught about incorrect facts or processes, individual experiences with error situations and the productive use of errors are necessary to acquire this type of knowledge (cf. Oser/Spychiger 2005).

In the literature, different possible mechanisms are described which give an idea as to how errors and the related negative knowledge can promote individual learning. For example, detecting and explaining an error helps to revise inaccurate knowledge structures (Ohlsson 1996). Moreover, an error experience can prevent the repetition of this error in similar situations because errors are salient and memorable (Jones/Endsley 2000). Both examples show that specific cognitive processes are necessary for learning from error situations. Specifically, four significant conditions can be postulated for learning in error situations (cf. Oser et al. 1999; Guldimann/Zutavern 1999). The learner must be able:

- to identify the error and its consequences (sensibility),
- to understand the error and to explain it (analysis),
- to correct the error (correction),
- and to develop strategies for avoiding similar errors (prevention)

The previous considerations about negative knowledge from a cognitive perspective indicate that errors have a positive role in learning processes. There is empirical evidence for this assumption from research on error management training in different domains of working life (for a meta-analysis see Keith/ Frese 2008).

Although the occurrence of errors can be considered as beneficial for learning processes, it cannot be ignored that the role of error experiences is a problematic one. Taking into account the affective perspective, errors are often considered as an indicator for individual failure. This means that they are experienced as a negative incident to be avoided. Hence, associating errors with negative feelings can be considered disadvantageous for cognitive learning processes, as students are likely to avoid situations in which errors may occur and avoid dealing with their errors in the manner that negative knowledge is acquired (Ames/Archer 1988; Nicholls 1984).

4.2.2 Error-handling Activities in the Mathematics Classroom

In this section, we give a short summary of empirical findings with respect to dealing with errors in a mathematics class. In particular, we present findings from classroom observations as well as from teacher and student surveys.

In terms of observational investigations of mathematics classes such as videotape studies, there are only few studies on the specific question of dealing with errors in mathematics lessons. Findings from video-based investigations from Switzerland (Oser et al. 1998, ten lessons from different grades in the lower secondary level), from the USA and Italy (Santagata 2005, 30 lessons from Grade 8 in each country) and Germany (Heinze 2004, 22 lessons from Grade 8) show similar tendencies in the four countries. Firstly, the number of errors in the public teacher-students interaction is comparatively low. On average, between three and five errors occur per mathematics lesson. Secondly, about 90% of the public handling of errors in mathematics lessons is clearly teacher-directed.[2] About a quarter to a third of the errors are corrected directly by the teacher, whereas about 50-60% of public students' errors are returned by the teacher to the students as a challenge.

Oser and Spychiger (2005) explain the low number of errors per mathematics lesson with error avoidance behavior of teachers and students. In particular, teachers try to avoid interruptions in the ongoing instruction process and do not want to expose students who make errors. Accordingly, they pose their questions in such a way that students rarely give erroneous answers.

This explanation is supported by findings from a series of interviews with Swiss mathematics teachers (Oser et al. 1999). It turned out that, on the one hand, teachers consider error handling as a natural part of teaching and they do not want to punish or expose students for their errors. However, on the other hand, they do not have clear strategies as to how to deal with errors in the lesson constructively. It seems as if they are unaware of the important role errors play in the learning process.

When it comes to the students' perspective on handling errors in a mathematics class, there are hardly any empirical studies with a clear focus on the topic. The Swiss group of Oser and colleagues developed a specific student questionnaire concerning error responses and collected data from 295 fourth to ninth grade students (Spychiger et al. 1998; Spychiger et al. 2006). The questionnaire consists of 27 items with three underlying factors: (1) teacher behavior in error situations, (2) the use of errors as individual learning opportunities, (3) emotional aspects of error situations. The results of the Swiss study indicate that students have a rather positive attitude toward dealing with errors made during a mathematics class, as well as toward the role their teachers play. Students perceive their teachers' dealing with errors made as friendly and supportive. The students seldom report anxiety due to mistakes made in mathematics class. However, students only show moderate results in their responses to "use of errors as individual learning opportunities".

4.3 Aims and Research Questions

With respect to the theory of negative knowledge, errors can be considered as an essential part of learning processes. Although errors have such a significance, they do not play a prominent role in the mathematics class. It seems that in several western countries teachers and students follow a latent behaviorist orientation in avoiding errors. In the reported Swiss study, the few situations of dealing with errors in mathematics lessons were rated compara-

---

[2] This applies to Germany, Italy and the U.S. There is no data for Switzerland.

tively positively by students in terms of emotional aspects and teacher behavior. Nevertheless, the findings indicate that these students do not consciously use their own errors as learning opportunities.

Our research aims to improve the existing empirical database and to get more insight into the relation between the teacher and student levels regarding dealing with errors in mathematics lessons. Based on empirical data from a large survey on handling errors in German mathematics classes, we specifically examine data representing the perspective of students. We assume that from the learners' perspective, the perception of dealing with errors during lessons is an important factor to explain students' behavior regarding the use of error situations as learning opportunities. Accordingly, our study is guided by the following research questions:

- How do students perceive the way in which their mathematics teachers handle errors? Do students fear making errors in these classes?
- How do students handle their own errors individually? Do they consider errors as learning opportunities?
- Is there a relationship between students' perceptions of their mathematics teachers' handling of errors and their own feelings regarding errors in mathematics, on the one hand, and their individual use of errors as learning opportunities on the other hand? Exactly what kind of teacher support is useful to reduce the fear of making errors and increase individual use of errors as learning opportunities?

4.4 Method

4.4.1 Sample

We analyzed students' perceptions of error handling in the mathematics classroom in an explorative study. The sample of this study involved 1674 students (791 female, 811 male)[3] from 74 classrooms in the metropolitan areas of two cities in the northern and southern parts of Germany. Data collection took place at different times in the school year, in different school types (comprehensive schools and schools from the academically focused school track 'Gymnasium'). We mainly chose classrooms from Grade 7. In Germany that is about two years after the transition from primary school to secondary school. In addition, there are some classrooms from Grades 6, 8 and 9 (see table 1).

Since we do not have a specific hypothesis about differences in students'

---

3   Gender was not reported by 72 students.

perceptions of error handling in the mathematics classroom in different grades or school types of the secondary level, we do not analyze the data in this respect.

Table 1: Structure of the sample

Grade (age)	Number of classes	Number of students
6 (12/13 years)	5	102
7 (13/14 years)	56	1309
8 (14/15 years)	11	223
9 (15/16 years)	2	40

Source: own table

4.4.2 Instruments and Procedure

A slightly adapted version of the Swiss questionnaire on error handling in the mathematics classroom with 26 items (Spychiger et al. 1998) was used to assess students' attitudes toward error-handling. Each item consisted of a statement which the students had to rate on a four point Likert scale. The adapted questionnaire was validated in a pilot survey with three classrooms which were not part of the sample. All questionnaires were administered in the classrooms by trained test assistants. The data collection procedure in each classroom took approximately 10 minutes.

To analyze the data of the questionnaire, a factor analysis (principal axis analysis with varimax rotation) was conducted. In contrast to the Swiss data set, which led to three factors (cf. section 4.2.2; Spychiger et al. 2006), we extracted a solution with four factors for our data. In particular, we could distinguish a factor describing perceived cognitive teacher support in using errors as a learning opportunity, and a factor of perceived affective teacher support in dealing with error situations in the classroom[4]. However, five teacher-related items can be interpreted from a cognitive as well as from an affective point of view and load on both factors. Though this strong common core in these two teacher factors exists, for theoretical purposes we have decided to separate these two factors. As mentioned in Section 4.2.1, cognitive and affective aspects each play a different role in error-handling situations. Accordingly, we expect that students' perception of their teachers' behavior with respect to affective and cognitive issues might have a different impact. The other two factors represent items referring to students' fear of making errors in mathematics lessons and their individual use of errors in the learning process, as can be seen in the factor solution of the Swiss group (Spychiger et al. 2006). Overall, the four factors solution explains 44.5% of

---

[4] As criteria we took into account the eigenvalues greater 1 and the screeplot.

the variance. Item examples and values for the reliability for all factors are given in Table 2. The reliability values (Cronbach's α) are acceptable for all four factors so that the associated item sets can be used as scales.

Table 2: Four Factors of the Student Questionnaire: Item Examples and Reliability[5]

Factor	Item example	Reliability (Cronbach's α)
Individual use of errors for the learning process	In mathematics I explore my errors and try to understand them.	.82 (9 items)
Affective aspects of teacher behavior in error situations	Sometimes our math teacher looks distressed when a student makes an error.	.87 (6 items)
Cognitive aspects of teacher behavior in error situations	If I make an error in maths lessons my teacher handles the situation in a way that I can benefit from.	.79 (4 items)
Fear of making errors in mathematics lessons	I become scared when I make an error in mathematics.	.76 (5 items)
Likert scale: 1 = strongly disagree, 2 = disagree, 3 = agree, 4 = strongly agree		

Source: own table

4.5 Results

4.5.1 Student Perceptions of Dealing with Errors in the Mathematics Class

To answer the first two research questions on students' perceptions of error-handling activities in the mathematics class, we consider the mean values of the four different factors. Regarding the factor *Fear of making errors in mathematics lessons* a mean value of $M = 1.87$ ($SD = 0.67$) suggests that students in our sample hardly fear making errors.[6] In line with this result, students also give the affective aspects of teacher behavior comparatively positive rating ($M = 3.01$, $SD = 0.79$). As the corresponding percentile band in fig. 1 shows, the students of our sample show quite a high level of agreement regarding these two factors. Only a small number of students report

---

[5] Two Items could not be assigned uniquely to one of the constructs due to inconsistent factor loadings and were omitted in this analysis.
[6] Unlike with the other factors, greater values do not represent a better situation for the factor *Fear of making errors in mathematics lessons*.

negative experiences with respect to affective attributes to error situations.

How do students individually handle their own errors? As we can see from the mean value of the factor *Individual use of errors for the learning process* (M = 2.52, SD = 0.57), there is no clear tendency showing students using their errors as learning opportunities. The corresponding percentile bands in figure 1 indicate that there is quite a large diversity in the sample. Here, we also have a relation to the teacher behavior, as it was reported for the affective attributes of error-handling situations. It seems that there is insufficient support from teachers for cognitive learning activities in error situations, since the mean value for the factor *Cognitive aspects of teacher behavior in error situations* is comparatively low (M = 2.73, SD = 0.76).

Figure 1: Error-handling in the mathematics class from the student perspective[7]

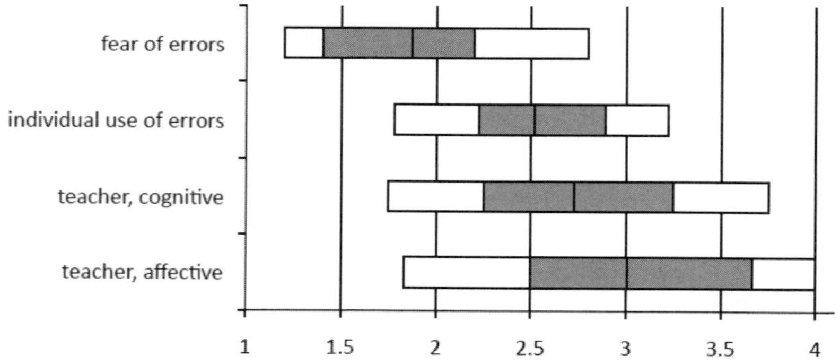

Source: own diagram

4.5.2 Hierarchical Regression Analyses

As the third research question indicates, one aim of this study is to analyze the relationships between a student's reported use of errors in the learning process, their fear of making errors in the mathematics classroom and their perception about their teacher's support in learning from errors. Perceived teacher behavior can be regarded as an indicator for atmosphere in the classroom, whereas reported use of errors for learning and reported fear of making errors can be seen as an indicator of classroom culture in respect to individual learning from errors. Thus, a hierarchical linear modeling procedure (HLM, Raudenbush/Bryk 2002) was applied to model effects on both an

---

7   The figure shows the 10%, 25%, 75%, and 90% percentiles as well as the mean values of average ratings on the items represented by each factor.

individual level and on a class level. This allows us to draw conclusions about teacher behavior and perceived classroom atmosphere (classroom level) as well as to analyze relations between perceived teacher behavior and student variables, for example fear of making errors and attitudes towards learning from errors (individual level). An analysis using "only" traditional regression models would not have accounted for the non-independence of observations caused by the nested sample of students in classrooms.

Analyses of the intraclass correlations (ICC) indicate that small to medium amounts of variance of the four factors can be explained by variation between classroom groups. Even though the between-classroom variation in students' reported fear of making errors and attitude towards learning from errors was not so large as to indicate that a multilevel analyses would be considered essential (9.9% of the variance for *fear of making errors in mathematics lessons* and 6.6% of the *variance for individual use of errors in the learning process*), the variance in reported teacher behavior was considerable (27.9% for cognitive aspects and 36.9% for affective aspects). Due to this variation in the predictors for individual feelings and attitudes, multilevel analyses are the most appropriate tool to differentiate between class-level and individual-level effects.

Table 3: Hierarchical regression analyses (standardized regression coefficients)

Dependent variable	**Fear of making errors**		**Individual use of errors**			
	Model 1		**Model 2**		**Model 3**	
Predictor	Classroom level	Individual level	Classroom level	Individual level	Classroom level	Individual level
Teacher behavior cognitive aspects	0.82***	0.10***	0.87***	0.39***	0.08$^{n.s.}$	0.37***
Teacher behavior affective aspects	-1.21***[8]	-0.42***	-0,26$^{n.s.}$	0,04$^{n.s.}$	0.90*	0.12***
Fear of making errors	---	---	---	---	0.97***	0.19***
R^2	0.61	0.14	0.47	0.17	0.84	0.20

*: p<.05; **: p<.01; ***: p<.001

Source: own table

Three hierarchical regression models were estimated. The first two analyze the effect of (perceived) teacher behavior on both students' feelings about, and attitude towards, learning from errors. Thus, the factors *affective aspects of teacher behavior in error situations* and *cognitive aspects of teacher be-*

---

[8] Estimates larger than one for (standardized) regression coefficients may result from correlated prediction variables (cf. Deegan 1978).

havior in error situations were used to predict the *individual use of errors in the learning process* and *fear of making errors in mathematics lessons* respectively.

As Models 1 and 2 indicate, the cognitive support from the teacher (in the perceptions of the students) plays an ambiguous role. On the one hand, it is connected to a more intensive use of errors for the learning process on the individual level as well as on the class level (Model 2). On the other hand, a perception of cognitive support from the teacher tends to occur concurrently with greater fear of making errors in the class, but this effect is only significant for the individual level (Model 1). Contrary to expectations, affective teacher support does not show a positive effect on the individual use of errors in the classroom (Model 2). Nevertheless, the hypothesized connection between perceived affective support and lower fear of making errors occurs on both classroom and individual level (Model 1). The variance explanation on the class-level is generally larger than on the individual level.

Though non-significant, the trend of negative effects of *affective aspects of teacher behavior in error situations* on *individual use of errors in the learning process* requires deeper analysis. To complete the picture, we consider a third hierarchical regression model (Model 3). The idea behind this analysis is that this effect should be a composition of a direct effect of *affective aspects of teacher behavior in error situations* on *individual use of errors in the learning process* and an indirect effect through the reduction of *fear of making errors*. Thus, fear of making errors is added as an additional predictor to Model 2. This model indicates a positive effect of both *affective aspects of teacher behavior in error situations* and *fear of making errors in mathematics lessons* on *individual use of errors in the classroom*, which is much more pronounced on the classroom level than on the individual level. Moreover, the effect of *cognitive aspects of teacher behavior in error situations* is no longer significant on the classroom level in this model. The amount of variance explained by the model substantially increased on the class level when including fear of making errors as an additional predictor, emphasizing that the relevant issue does not seem to be the individual fear of making mathematical errors, but rather the corresponding atmosphere created in the classroom.

4.5.3 Interpretation of Hierarchical Regression Results

Since our sample is comprised of students from 74 classrooms, the empirical data has a nested structure. Accordingly, a multi-level analysis is necessary to investigate the influence of the classroom level on individual variables. A significant but small influence of the classroom level on the factors *individual use of errors in the classroom* and *fear of making errors in mathematics lessons* (about 10% and 7% explained variance respectively) became apparent. It seems that the teacher and other classroom variables only have a minor impact on these factors on the student level. In contrast to this, for both teacher factors (affective and cognitive) there is a more significant impact from the classroom level (for *cognitive aspects of teacher behavior in error situations* 27.9% and for *affective aspects of teacher behavior in error situations* 36.9% of the explained variance).[9] Nevertheless, a large amount of variance is still caused by inter-individual differences.

In some aspects the predictor pattern found in our study is as expected. Cognitive aspects of teacher support show a strong relation to the use of errors as a learning opportunity on the classroom and individual level, indicating the hypothesized positive effect of a cognitively activating, supportive classroom climate. In principle, this is a favorable result since it points towards possibilities of supportive classroom practice.

Nevertheless, this very same aspect of teacher behavior is also connected to fear of making errors. Individual students might easily perceive cognitive activation when an error occurs – no matter how supportively intended – as an additional demand imposed by the teacher. If adequate autonomy support is missing, this additional demand can lead to a connection of error-making with negative emotions (Hugener et al. 2009; Pekrun et al. 2002). This interpretation is in line with the fact that the effect is much more pronounced on the classroom level. Regarding affective outcomes of classroom instruction, this effect is nevertheless unsatisfactory.

An astonishing result in the first instance is the missing effect of affective teacher support on individual use of errors in the classroom. A deeper analysis which takes fear of errors into account clarifies the picture: Fear of making errors is – given constant cognitive and affective teacher support – connected to a more intense use of errors in the learning process. It can be assumed that this correspondence cannot be generalized into high levels of fear. Nevertheless, the possible activating effects of certain negative emotions (like fear) are discussed in the literature (e.g. Pekrun et al. 2002). With growing fear of errors it can be expected that use of errors in the learning process will decline finally, leading to the hypothesis of an inverse-U-shaped relation. For our sample, the activating effect of fear seems to be dominant.

Given this unexpected activating effect of fear, the non-significant effect of affective teacher support in Model 2 can be interpreted. Increased affective teacher support is connected to an increase of individual use of errors directly, as expected. This effect is inhibited, however, by an indirect effect: increased affective teacher support reduces fear of making errors, which plays the role of an activating emotion in this case.

All these effects of fear of making errors and affective teacher support are

---

9   Please note that both factors have a common core of five items (as described earlier).

generally more pronounced on classroom level. This indicates that they are largely caused by the corresponding atmosphere in the classroom, rather than by individual perceptions of teacher behavior. Nevertheless, the activating effect of fear leaves the educator with an uneasy feeling about educational implications here.

There is a bright side when considering the individual use of errors as a learning opportunity: at least on the individual level, the individual use of errors can be positively influenced by supportive teacher behavior with regard to cognitive aspects. This effect is however dominant on the individual level, indicating that this cognitive teacher support does not generate a corresponding atmosphere in the classroom that affects all students equally. Whether this is a general problem of cognitive support, or if it can be changed by adequate interventions is an empirical question that cannot be answered here.

4.6 Discussion

Errors play an important role in the learning process. Proverbs in many languages give evidence that this is common knowledge in cultures all over the world. For teaching and learning in school and, in particular, in the mathematics classroom, errors are often considered as a part of the learning process in the sense of a (negative) concomitant phenomenon. It seems that many teachers are not aware of the important cognitive (and affective) role which errors play in knowledge acquisition. Accordingly, teachers try to handle errors in such a way that students are not affected by negative emotions. Moreover, as video-studies indicate, there is a tendency to avoid errors in the mathematics class.

The consequence is that students indeed acknowledge their teacher's positive behavior with respect to emotional aspects but not with respect to cognitive aspects. Our results show that the emotional aspects of error situations in the mathematics class are given a comparatively positive rating by the students: they hardly have any fear of making errors and they agree that the error-handling of their teachers is quite good from the affective point of view. The cognitive aspects of error situations must be regarded more critically. The cognitive support of teachers in error situations is rated worse than the affective aspects of the teacher behavior. Moreover, there is no clear tendency that students use their errors as learning opportunities.

The results of the multilevel analysis indicate that the relation between classroom variables and individual emotions about and attitudes toward errors in the learning process is characterized by a complex interplay of individual processes and aspects of the classroom atmosphere – specifically, the use of errors as a learning opportunity can be efficiently stimulated by cognitive teacher support. This support turns out, however, to be at th

e risk of an increased fear of making errors, should adequate support be missing. Furthermore, to some extent affective teacher support is suitable to create a positive classroom atmosphere, though at the risk of spoiling a possible activating role of fear of errors. Whether this activating role of fear is a desirable means of classroom instruction is a different ethical question that will not be discussed here. It can be hypothesized that a more detailed analysis of the individual and classroom characteristics studied here with further student variables like interest, academic self-concept, and mathematics achievement is necessary for a better understanding of this complex interplay.

Nevertheless, at this point some concrete implications can be drawn from our study:

- Creating an error-tolerant atmosphere by e.g. not reacting harshly may provide affective support for students when dealing with individual errors. This support is well suited to reduce fear of making errors in the classroom.
- To stimulate students to use errors as a learning opportunity, however, affective support in the sense of a warm positive climate with respect to errors does not seem to be sufficient. Activities to develop cognitive strategies to learn from error (like correcting the error, self-explaining why it is wrong, developing avoidance-strategies) are necessary.
- Fear of errors in the classroom plays an ambiguous role in that it seems – to a certain degree – to stimulate cognitive activities dealing with errors. It raises an important question as to whether the reduction of this stimulating effect caused by affective teacher support can be (over-)compensated by cognitive teacher support.

Finally, two major drawbacks of our study must be mentioned. Firstly, its cross-sectional design makes causal interpretations problematic. Secondly, teacher behavior was evaluated indirectly by students' perceptions. While the second problem might be solved with video studies, this complicated method would not be adequate to tackle the first issue. To get more sound results in this respect, planned intervention studies would be necessary. On the other hand, large sample sizes are necessary to be able to disentangle effects of classroom atmosphere from processes on the individual level.

Summarizing our findings, we can assume that German mathematics teachers show similar behavior to that of the Swiss teachers described in Section 4.2.2. Errors are considered a natural part of the learning process and a negative connotation should be avoided in the classroom. Our results indicate that German teachers are successful in this respect. However, it seems that they do not have instructional strategies on how to use errors in the lessons productively and how to teach their students to use their errors as learning opportunities. Regarding the nature of adequate teacher interventions, some first ideas can be drawn from our analyses. Nevertheless, further research is necessary to clarify the interplay of cognitive and affective aspects on individual and classroom level.

References

Ames, C./Archer, J. (1988): Achievement goals in the classroom: Students' learning strategies and motivation processes. In: *Journal of Educational Psychology*, 80, pp. 260-267.
Bauer, J./Mulder, R. (2007): Modelling learning from errors in daily work. In: *Learning in Health and Social Care*, 6, 3, pp. 121-133.
Deegan, J. (1978): On the occurrence of standardized regression coefficients greater than one. In: *Educational and Psychological Measurement*, 38, pp. 873-888.
Guldimann, T./Zutavern, M. (1999): „Das passiert uns nicht noch einmal!" Schülerinnen und Schüler lernen gemeinsam den bewussten Umgang mit Fehlern. In: Althof, W. (ed.): *Fehlerwelten. Vom Fehlermachen und Lernen aus Fehlern*. Opladen: Leske + Budrich, pp. 233-258.
Heinze, A. (2004): Zum Umgang mit Fehlern im Unterrichtsgespräch der Sekundarstufe I. In: *Journal für Mathematik-Didaktik*, 25, 3/4, pp. 221-244.
Hugener, I./Pauli, C./Reusser, K./Lipowsky, F./Rakoczy, K./Klieme, E. (2009): Teaching patterns and learning quality in Swiss and German mathematics lessons. In: *Learning and Instruction*, 19, pp. 66-78.
Jones, D.G./Endsley, M.R. (2000): Overcoming representational errors in complex environments. In: *Human Factors*, 42, pp. 367-378.
Keith, N./Frese, M. (2008): Effectiveness of error management training: A meta-analysis. In: *Journal of Applied Psychology*, 93, 1, pp. 59-69.
Minsky, M. (1994): Negative expertise. In: *International Journal of Expert Systems*, 7, 1, pp. 13-19.
Nicholls, J.G. (1984): Conceptions of ability and achievement motivation. In: Ames, R./Ames, C. (eds.): *Research on Motivation in Education, Vol. 1, Student Motivation*. New York: Academic Press, pp. 39-73.
Ohlsson, S. (1996): Learning from performance errors. In: *Psychological Review*, 103, pp. 241-262.
Oser, F./Hascher, T./Spychiger, M. (1999): Lernen aus Fehlern. Zur Psychologie des „negativen" Wissens. In: Althof, W. (ed.): *Fehlerwelten. Vom Fehlermachen und Lernen aus Fehlern*. Opladen: Leske + Budrich, pp. 11-41.
Oser, F./Spychiger, M. (2005): *Lernen ist schmerzhaft. Zur Theorie des Negativen Wissens und zur Praxis der Fehlerkultur*. Weinheim: Beltz.
Oser, F./Spychiger, M./Mahler, F./Gut, K./Hascher, T./Büeler, U./Müller, V. (1998): *Lernen Menschen aus Fehlern? Zur Entwicklung einer Fehlerkultur in der Schule*. Scientific report (unpublished).

Pekrun, R./Goetz, T./Titz, W./Perry, R.P. (2002): Academic emotions in students' self-regulated learning and achievement: A program of qualitative and quantitative research. In: *Educational Psychologist,* 37, pp. 91-105.
Raudenbush, S.W./Bryk, A.S. (2002): *Hierarchical linear models: Applications and data analysis methods.* 2nd edn., Newbury Park, CA: Sage.
Reason, J. (1995): Understanding adverse events: human factors. In: *Quality in Health Care,* 4, pp. 80-89.
Santagata, R. (2005): Practices and beliefs in mistake-handling activities: A video study of Italian and U.S. mathematics lessons. In: *Teaching and Teacher Education,* 21, 5, pp. 491-508.
Spychiger, M./Kuster, R./Oser, F. (2006): Dimensionen von Fehlerkultur in der Schule und deren Messung. Der Schülerfragebogen zur Fehlerkultur im Unterricht für Schülerinnen und Schüler der Mittel- und Oberstufe. In: *Schweizerische Zeitschrift für Bildungswissenschaften,* 28, 1, pp. 87-110.
Spychiger, M./Mahler, F./Hascher, T./Oser, F. (1998): Fehlerkultur aus der Sicht von Schülerinnen und Schülern. Der Fragebogen S-UFS: Entwicklung und erste Ergebnisse. Research Report (unpublished).

5 Negative Knowledge of Primary School Teachers – Results from an Explorative Study

Martin Gartmeier, Katharina Lorenzer, Hans Gruber and Helmut Heid

5.1 Introduction

Young teachers have attended school for up to 13 years, have undergone didactical and pedagogical courses at university and have gained their first teaching experiences during teaching internships. Nonetheless, most teachers feel like they are thrown in at the deep end when starting out on their career. A cause for this experience, often referred to as *praxis shock* (Kelchtermans/ Ballet 2002), might be "discrepancies between teachers' expectations of school life and the realities of teaching" (Ballantyne 2007: 181).

For several reasons, this is a very critical situation: in the early years of their teaching career, teachers establish routines and practices which they may adhere to throughout their professional life. Moreover, they start to form their professional identity and professional role as well as their attitudes towards teaching (Flores 2001; Watzke 2007; Wideen/Mayer-Smith/Moon 1998). Hence, it is an especially important task for educational scientists to better understand the nature of the learning processes and experiences that young teachers have to go through. Deeper insights in this regard could serve as a basis for a better coordination between teacher education at university and the everyday requirements of the teaching profession. This, in turn, may enable better preparation of teachers for the challenges in the early stages of their career.

Seeking to make a contribution here, we draw upon the theory of negative knowledge (Gartmeier/Bauer/Gruber/Heid 2008; Oser/Spychiger 2005; Parviainen/Eriksson 2006). As will be argued below in more detail, negative knowledge is conceptualized as a form of experiential knowledge that is focused upon actions or action conditions that endanger the attainment of certain goals. Here is an example: almost every German pupil is confronted with a rule of thumb when learning about fractional arithmetic, namely 'to reduce a sum would just be dumb'. This rule does not contain any information about what to actually do when handling fractions. Its helpfulness with regard to pupils' mathematical competence lies in addressing a very common mistake in this context. The given example focuses upon negative knowledge that is helpful for pupils; yet, our focus here is teachers' negative knowledge about their own teaching practice. The key argument pursued by the negative knowledge approach is that being aware of possible (or probable) mistakes is a plausible prerequisite for their future avoidance. In this contribution, we investigate to what extent teachers use negative knowledge to describe their strategy for solving various hypothetical practice situations.

We have argued above that young teachers often face difficulties while establishing their routines and practices at school. In such situations, young teachers are confronted with the wrongness of their own assumptions about how to solve problems at work. This means they are urged to learn from their own errors (Bauer 2008) and to develop negative knowledge about how *not* to solve certain problems at work. Hence, it could be assumed that it is mainly young teachers who make extensive use of negative knowledge to describe their work practice. On the other hand, more experienced teachers have had more opportunities to learn from their work experience and to develop extensive experiential and negative knowledge.

However, we assume negative knowledge to be a particularly helpful resource for teachers due to its focus on critical situations (such as errors) at work and, similarly, due to its function for action regulation. Drawing upon these assumptions, our contribution pursues two goals: firstly, we investigate to what extent teachers with different levels of experience make use of negative knowledge to explain how they solve problems at work. Secondly, we compare different ways of acquiring negative knowledge in terms of their importance. These issues are addressed based on the results of a prompting-task study that was conducted with 35 primary school teachers. Before we describe this study and discuss its results, we will use the subsequent pages to introduce the theory of negative knowledge and to make clear why we believe that negative knowledge is valuable for young teachers.

5.2 Theoretical Background

5.2.1 *Negative Knowledge and Professional Competence*

Negative knowledge is defined as experientially acquired knowledge about assumptions that are wrong, but tend to be considered true. These assumptions might, e.g. have a factual (declarative) character ('Rio is *not* the capital of Brasil!') or action-oriented (procedural) character ('To reduce a sum would just be dumb!') (Gartmeier et al. 2008; Minsky 1994; Oser/Spychiger 2005). Both these forms of negative knowledge are closely connected to learning from errors at work. Errors at work are conceptualized as a category of adverse events that produce 'stress, accidents, inefficient human-machine interaction, quality and performance problems, and a bad climate' (Rybowiak et al. 1999: 528). When individuals learn from errors, they become aware of incorrect conceptions or erroneous work processes that they have adhered to. Learning from errors can thus be understood as the establishment of negative imperatives (Assumption X is wrong; Solving problem Y in this way yields poor outcomes). These imperatives address incorrect assumptions or routines that may cause workplace errors. Thus, negative knowledge may be a valuable part of an individual's practical knowledge, because it contains guidelines for avoiding similar errors in future practice.

The negative knowledge approach can be subsumed under more general conceptions of knowledge representation typically used in research on the knowledge of experts. In this field, script theories have been used for modelling the representation of experts' action-oriented knowledge (Schank 1999). Scripts are generalized action schemata that guide action in specific situations (e.g. the typical sequence of actions when visiting a restaurant) and that may comprise elements of declarative as well as procedural knowledge (Anderson/ Lebiere 1998). Scripts may change dynamically with the experience of new episodes. An important script-modification practice is the integration of deviant episodes into existing scripts (Kolodner 1983; Schank 1999). Hence, learning from errors can be interpreted as a process of extending an existing script with instances where its application was unsuccessful and with possible explanations for this deviance (Bauer 2008). These extensions may assist professional actions in future similar situations by reminding the actor of the failed episode, of possible explanations for the failure and of alternative ways of acting.

Of course this is an idealistic description of how existing scripts are modified based on the experience of deviant episodes. In fact, researchers have identified multiple factors that influence whether errors are actually learned from, e.g. the extent to which employees are willing to expose errors they have made and – connected to that – the possibility of being able to openly discuss one's errors with colleagues (Edmondson 1999).

However, the idea of negative knowledge fits neatly into the theory of scripts as a more comprehensive framework to represent action-oriented knowledge. One could conceive negative knowledge as being represented in those parts of scripts which refer to conditions that would probably cause failures in task attainment.

To sum up, negative knowledge is experiential knowledge focused on assumptions that turned out to be wrong or problem-solving strategies that were found to be unsuccessful. In order to substantiate the research questions posed here, the subsequent paragraphs will focus on how negative knowledge is applied by teachers with different levels of experience and on how it is acquired.

5.2.2 Application of Negative Knowledge

Our first research question focuses on the extent to which teachers with different levels of experience make use of negative knowledge to explain how they solve problems at work. It has been argued earlier that negative knowledge has a valuable problem-solving function in specific task situations because it reminds workers of potential error sources and therefore helps avoid them (Oser/Spychiger 2005). We assume that professionals in any given domain have a situation-specific repertoire of negative rules that make them anticipate particular errors and assist in the avoidance of these errors (Gartmeier et al. 2008; Kolodner 1983; Minsky 1994). Being aware of what actions are wrong in order to solve a given problem can be useful in order to establish an idea about what actions might be appropriate for doing so. This especially applies in situations which carry a fair chance of making errors or in which doing something wrong may result in serious consequences (Reason 1990). This assumption is consistent with arguments from research on case-based reasoning showing that analogies from cases previously experienced are helpful in mastering subsequent similar situations in that they remind an actor of what to avoid (Kolodner 1997).

For the present study, we investigate the extent to which teachers with different levels of experience apply negative knowledge when describing how they would act in various classroom situations. A study by Gartmeier, Lehtinen, Gruber and Heid (2011) pursued a similar goal while investigating care nurses for the elderly. There, largely different patterns were found through comparing professionals with different experience levels in the amount of declarative and procedural negative knowledge they used. For the present study, these facets of knowledge shall also be analysed separately.

Firstly, we assume that novice teachers will use declarative negative knowledge more extensively than their more experienced colleagues. This is because they have only recently finished their studies at university where they have acquired much declarative knowledge, especially while preparing for their final exams. Of course, more experienced teachers also have much declarative knowledge from different sources other than university. Yet we assume that they will more strongly rely upon their experience-based action-oriented knowledge than on their factual knowledge. This is in line with the results from Gartmeier et al. (2011) and also Strasser (2006).

Secondly, as was mentioned above, we assume that highly experienced teachers will exhibit more procedural negative knowledge than young teachers. As will become obvious, our study participants primarily reflect upon everyday classroom situations. It is conceivable that more experienced professionals have experienced more of these situations and hence know more about what to do – and what to avoid – in these situations (Bromme/Rambow/ Sträßer 1996).

5.2.3 Acquisition of Negative Knowledge

The second goal our study pursues is to compare different ways of acquiring negative knowledge in terms of their importance. In general, although educational settings can teach what should be avoided in the performance of a task, we assume personal experience to be potentially more powerful in the acquisition of negative knowledge (Oser/Spychiger 2005). An experience may serve as a starting point for the acquisition of negative knowledge, especially in cases that raise an actor's awareness of having inappropriate assumptions or applying inappropriate strategies for solving a problem at hand. Typically, errors at work are seen as experiences that meet this description as they provide opportunities to reflect on their causes and thereby gain insights that may allow for the avoidance of similar errors in future practice (Gartmeier et al. 2008; Bauer 2008; van Woerkom 2003). The results of such reflective processes contribute to building a body of negative knowledge concerning what should be avoided in a given class of work situations.

On the basis of these assumptions, our second hypothesis is that personal experience and informal learning are far more important sources for acquiring negative knowledge than formal learning.

5.3 Method

5.3.1 Sample

The study respondents were 35 primary school teachers from Bavarian elementary schools. The respondents' professional experience ranged from 0 to 37 years with an average of 11.46 ($SD = 13.07$) years; their age averaged 37.2 ($SD = 13.68$). With regard to our goal of comparing teachers with different levels of experience, we separately investigated three groups: firstly, respondents with up to two years of teaching experience (13 individuals). The members of this group are in the final period of their teacher studies and hence are not yet fully appointed teachers. Secondly, professionals whose experience ranged between three and nine years (seven individuals) were questioned. Thirdly, highly experienced professionals with tenure of ten or more years (15 study participants) were involved. The criterion for differentiating the two latter-mentioned groups is the 10-year rule of necessary preparation (Bromme 1992; Ericsson 1996). In the following paragraphs, the three groups will be addressed as *grp0-2*; *grp3-9*, *grp10+*. Our sample comprised six male teachers and 29 female teachers.

5.3.2 Instruments and Procedures

Data was collected by means of the prompting-task methodology (Brewer 1986; Crovitz/Schiffman 1974; Custers/Boshuizen/Schmidt 1996). In this structured interview technique, cognitive content is activated through prompts upon which the subjects reflect. In this study, 20 everyday teaching situations served as prompts. These were developed in a pre-study with one expert and one semi-expert teacher who kept a diary over three weeks about classroom situations that they perceived as being challenging for the teacher. From these diaries, a list of 20 critical classroom situations was developed. In the interviews, the situations were presented as short texts on a laptop screen. Here are two examples: *"You enter the classroom and read the hugely written sentence 'Martina is a fat cow!' on the blackboard"*. Another prompted hypothetical situation was as follows: *"Mobile phones are forbidden in your school. In class, you catch a student typing an SMS underneath the desk. You confiscate the phone and put it on your desk. Some minutes later, the phone is gone"*. The list of situations was reviewed by further different expert teachers and was further modified according to their recommendations. With every situation, the same two questions were posed: *What would be wrong ways for a teacher to act in this situation? And what would you describe as the most important source of your knowledge?* The respondents were given no time limit for answering.

In the first phase of data analysis, a category scheme was developed to capture the different facets of the teachers' negative knowledge. Through several discussions among the authors of this paper, the category scheme was improved and refined. For calculating the inter-rater reliability, two raters independently applied the final version of the category scheme to a random sample of 10 % of the interviews (i.e., four interviews). A score of Cohen's κ = 0.61 was calculated. For the quantitative analyses reported below, the frequency of the codings was counted and the three expertise groups were compared by means of unifactorial ANOVAs.

5.4 Results

All interviews were tape-recorded and transcribed verbally. The identification of negative knowledge occurred by means of a content-analytic approach. In cases where statements could not be identified unambiguously as representing negative knowledge or where particular statements did not clearly relate to one of the subcategories, the concerns were resolved in discussions between the authors of this paper. As was described above, our analysis focused on two forms of negative knowledge, namely declarative factual negative knowledge (how something is not) and procedural action-related negative knowledge (what not to do in a certain situation). The average duration of an interview was 18:27 minutes. The longest interviews with a mean duration of 22:45 minutes ($M = 16:45$, $M = 17:56$) were recorded among the *grp3-9* individuals. On average, *grp3-9* individuals made the most statements of negative knowledge ($M = 51.57$; $SD = 19.09$) followed by the *grp0-3* individuals ($M = 42.92$, $SD = 16.24$). The group with the highest amount of work experience (*grp10+*) uttered the least negative knowledge ($M = 40.00$; $SD = 15.34$) – yet with only a small average difference to the novice group and no systematic differences between the groups.

As was indicated, the two forms of negative knowledge differentiated in our study were procedural and declarative negative knowledge. In the procedural understanding of negative knowledge, the subjects reflected about what not to do. Thereby, they mainly described incidents of suboptimal professional behaviour (e.g. *"When writing the school certificate, I have to pay attention not to write too complicated in order for the pupils to understand what is meant; on the other hand, it still has to be informative for the parents as well"*). In contrast, the subjects' declarative negative knowledge focused on how something is not. This type of negative knowledge was used to label assumptions which could be wrong in the situations, e.g.: *"The phone being gone does not mean that the pupil that I took it from has taken it"* (This statement relates to the latter situation exemplified above). In terms of the acquisition of negative knowledge, we differentiated between formal and informal learning as sources of knowledge. The following statements were labelled as formal contexts of knowledge acquisition: university courses; studying educational literature; attending seminars; and professional-development courses. The following answers were categorized as informal contexts of acquiring negative knowledge: own reflection on problems and challenges at work; observation of colleagues; daily routine; experience from the internship, traineeship; experience as a pupil; intuition; experience from being a parent.

The first major task of this study was to compare teachers with different levels of experience in terms of the amounts of declarative and procedural negative knowledge that they mention in our study. Therefore, univariate ANOVAs were conducted. These showed a significant difference in declarative negative knowledge (cf. Table 1). Here, semi-experts show significantly more declarative negative knowledge than novices or experts. These results will be discussed below.

Table 1: Differences between negative knowledge in the three experience groups

Means
(Standard deviations)

	(1) Grp0-2	(2) Grp3-9	(3) Grp10+	Standard error	F	post hoc
Nk	42.92 (16.24)	51.57 (19.09)	40.00 (15.34)	2.79	1.19	
D_Nk	13.15 (10.16)	23.71 (24.30)	14.13 (16.91)	2.80	1.04*	2>3.1
P_Nk	29.77 (21.13)	27.86 (30.11)	25.87 (20.23)	3.74	0.10	

Note: Nk = Negative knowledge (overall); D_Nk = declarative negative knowledge; P_Nk = procedural negative knowledge; For all F-Tests df = (2). *: $p < .10$; **: $p < .05$; ***: $p < .01$; η^2 = effect size.

Source: own table

Our second goal was to identify which context plays a more important role for acquiring negative knowledge – the formal or the informal context. Table 2 shows that the informal context ($\sum = 55.17$) was named more often than the formal context ($\sum = 19.9$) as a place for acquiring negative knowledge.

Table 2: Teachers with different levels of experience's estimations of the importance of the formal and the informal context for acquiring negative knowledge

Means
(Standard deviations)

	(1) Grp0-2	(2) Grp3-9	(3) Grp10+	Standard error	F	posthoc
IC	16.38 (4.79)	21.14 (5.64)	17.20 (4.90)	0.87	2.178	-
FC	6.92 (3.38)	6.71 (6.52)	6.27 (3.33)	0.68	0.09	-

Note: IC = Informal context; FC = Formal context; For all F-Tests df = (2). *: $p < .10$; **: $p < .05$; ***: $p < .01$; η^2 = effect size.

Source: own table

Furthermore, Table 2 shows that semi-experts more often mention informal contexts as being relevant for acquiring negative knowledge than the other groups. In contrast, the formal context is mentioned by all groups in our study to almost the same extent. In comparison, formal learning contexts seem to offer much less opportunities for acquiring negative knowledge than informal ones.

5.5 Discussion

Teachers of all experience levels mentioned negative knowledge in the course of our interviews. This is a positive result with regard to our assumption of the relevance of this form of knowledge in the teacher's everyday practice and it encourages further inquiry on this issue.

However, some limitations need to be addressed in view of future inquiry into negative knowledge: one concern related to the present study is that it does not incorporate a measure to determine the quality of the study participants' actual success in resolving the described classroom situations. Accordingly, the assumption that the amount and quality of the individual's negative knowledge has an impact on the quality of professional performance delivered is merely theoretical and cannot be empirically verified based on the results provided here (Whyte/Ward/Eccles 2009). What follows is that one perspective for future studies would be to combine measures of a person's negative knowledge with indicators of performance in mastering specific tasks. Such indicators could also be useful in order to establish a sounder basis for differentiating between different groups of individuals in the investigated sample. We have used professional experience as a criterion, whereas some current approaches in research on expertise pursue multicriterial approaches (Ericsson/Whyte/Ward 2007).

One result of our study was that the group of moderately experienced teachers expressed more declarative negative knowledge than very young as well as very experienced teachers. As was argued above, declarative negative knowledge is focused on how something is not, e.g., in the sense of non-similarities between different phenomena. Hence, it may be helpful for avoiding incorrect interpretations of certain situations (Gartmeier/Gruber/Heid 2010; Oser/Spychiger 2005). The result of the moderately experienced group of teachers showing the most negative knowledge of this focus is somewhat unusual. In general, a nonlinear pattern emerging from the comparison of different expertise groups is known as an intermediate effect, which manifests as "a learning curve or developmental pattern that is shaped like either a U or an inverted U" (Patel/Ramoni 1997: 92). However, the inverted U is the more common result. It has been explained as drawing upon the encapsulation theory (Boshuizen/Schmidt 1992), which assumes that along with growing professional experience and the application of knowledge in many cases, it is organized in situation-specific script-like structures. These allow for solving common problems without having to explicitly consider the underlying knowledge. Yet this knowledge can be consulted if uncommon problems appear. This explanation is applicable to the present results: the group of moderately experienced teachers (*grp3-9*) under investigation here are the ones who – compared to their younger colleagues – have collected more experience and have abstracted their experiences to a higher degree. This allows them to apply more negative knowledge to the given situations. Moreover – compared to older colleagues – these rules have not yet become such an integral part of their routines. It seems that for the middle group, negative declarative knowledge is most helpful as a means to describe critical classroom circumstances and as a guideline to their teaching behaviour.

Despite the plausibility of this effect, it has to be said that the empirical foundation provided through the present study is not fully satisfying. Due to the small sample size and the significance being only on the 10% level, future studies should investigate whether this effect can be replicated. However, no further systematic differences between teachers with different levels of experience of negative knowledge could be identified. This might be due to two points: firstly, we should have interviewed more individuals; secondly, the differences in the sizes of the three experience groups should have been smaller. It is a rarely contended phenomenon that larger sample sizes increase the chances of hypotheses confirmation (Rasch/Friese/Hofmann/Naumann 2006). More importantly, the group of moderately experienced teachers is somewhat underrepresented in our study compared to the other groups. Another critical issue in the study concerns the differentiation between the expertise groups: especially in the group of semi-experts, it seems plausible that large differences exist between individuals with three and those with nine years of experience. A proximate action would be to further divide this group into subgroups. Yet, in the present study, the group of semi-experts consists of only seven individuals. Dividing this group would further decrease the number of individuals in each group – which, in turn, would further decrease the probability of detecting systematic differences.

Concerning research question two, our results are as expected. The informal context showed itself to be a far more relevant source for acquiring negative knowledge than the formal context. This is in line with the characterization of personal experience being the primary source of negative knowledge (Gartmeier et al. 2008). Of course, one weakness of this result is the fact that teachers themselves described how they have acquired their knowledge – and this is not trivial.

With regard to teacher education programs, the latter result stresses two things: firstly, teachers should be given the opportunity to have authentic experiences in the very early stages of their teaching career. Secondly, teacher education programs should systematically use these experiences and guide teachers in reflecting upon them and in drawing inferences from these experiences. Experiencing oneself in challenging situations can teach one about one's own strengths and weaknesses and can hence provide invaluable information about what is still to be learned in order to be a good teacher (Prenzel 2010).

5.6 Conclusion

The argument that opened this chapter was that negative knowledge can be regarded as a valuable resource for young teachers experiencing a praxis shock. This is because such knowledge contains information that may be relevant in order to avoid certain mistakes. Teacher education programs which combine authentic and challenging experiences with opportunities for reflection upon these experiences should support teachers in developing negative knowledge from the very early stages of their professional education.

As for future research on negative knowledge, it is important to raise the question as to how instructional settings should be designed in order to foster its development. This, of course, does not mean that teachers in training should solely be taught what to avoid in teaching practice. Most importantly, teachers should be able to act professionally and to provide effective instruction to the pupils they work with. Thereby, it is helpful to also be aware of what does not work. In the best of cases, having negative knowledge means having made errors, having reflected upon these errors and thereby having gained insight into instructional strategies that work for oneself in practice and strategies that do not work.

Researching negative knowledge therefore means acknowledging that learning about how to act in a complex professional domain can never be understood as a process of merely accumulating a body of simple rules, such as if you face problem X, then apply strategy Y. Instead, it is a complex process of trying out things – ideally based on one's previous knowledge about instructional theories and didactics – of evaluating the results of one's attempts and of modifying more general principles which are followed. From this perspective, it is only natural that some of these principles will turn out to be inappropriate in order to provide effective instruction. This characterization makes clear why Oser and Spychiger (2005) describe learning as being painful on the one hand and why they see negative knowledge as an inevitable result – yet also invaluable one – on the other.

References

Anderson, J./Lebiere, C. (1998): *The atomic components of thought.* Mahwah: Erlbaum.

Ballantyne, J. (2007): Documenting praxis shock in early-career Australian music teachers: The impact of pre-service teacher education. In: *International Journal of Music Education*, 25, pp. 181-191.

Bauer, J. (2008): *Learning from errors at work. Studies on nurses' engagement in error related learning activities.* Dissertation, University of Regensburg. Retrieved April 4, 2011, from http://epub.uni-regensburg.de/10748/1/diss_veroeff_endversion.pdf.

Boshuizen, H. P. A./Schmidt, H. G. (1992): On the role of biomedical knowledge in clinical reasoning by experts, intermediates and novices. In: *Cognitive Science*, 16, pp. 153-184.

Brewer, W. F. (1986): What is autobiographical memory? In Rubin, D. (ed.): *Autobiographical memory.* New York: Cambridge University Press, pp. 25-49.

Bromme, R. (1992): *Der Lehrer als Experte. Zur Psychologie des professionellen Wissens.* Bern: Huber.

Bromme, R./Rambow, R./Sträßer, R. (1996): Jenseits von ‚Oberfläche' und ‚Tiefe': Zum Zusammenhang von Problem-kategorisierungen und Arbeitskontext bei Fachleuten des Technischen Zeichnens. In: Gruber, H./Ziegler, A. (eds.): *Expertiseforschung: Theoretische und methodische Grundlagen.* Opladen: Westdeutscher Verlag, pp. 150-168.

Crovitz, H. F./Schiffman, H. (1974): Frequency of episodic memories as a function of their age. In: *Bulletin of the Psychonomic Society*, 4, pp. 517-518.

Custers, E. J. F. M./Boshuizen, H. P. A./Schmidt, H. G. (1996): The influence of medical expertise, case typicality, and illness script component on case processing and disease probability estimates. In: *Memory & Cognition*, 24, pp. 384-399.

Edmondson, A. C. (1999): Psychological safety and learning behavior in work teams. In: *Administrative Science Quarterly*, 44, pp. 350-383.

Ericsson, K. A. (ed.) (1996): *The road to excellence: the acquisition of expert performance in the arts and sciences, sports, and games.* Mahwah: Erlbaum.

Ericsson, K. A./Whyte, J./Ward, P. (2007): Expert performance in nursing: Reviewing research on expertise in nursing within the framework of the expert performance approach. In: *Advances in Nursing Science*, 30, E58-E71.

Flores, M. A. (2001): Person and context in becoming a new teacher. In: *Journal of Education for Teaching*, 27, pp. 135-148.

Gartmeier, M./Bauer, J./Gruber, H./Heid, H. (2008): Negative knowledge: Understanding professional learning and expertise. In: *Vocations and Learning*, 1, pp. 87–103.

Gartmeier, M./Gruber, H./Heid, H. (2010): Tracing error-related knowledge in interview data: Negative knowledge in elder care nursing. In: *Educational Gerontology*, 36, pp. 733-752.

Gartmeier, M./Lehtinen, E./Gruber, H./Heid, H. (2011): Negative expertise: Comparing differently experienced elder care nurses' negative knowledge. In: *European Journal of Psychology of Education*, 26, pp. 273-300.

Kelchtermans, G./Ballet, K. (2002): The micropolitics of teacher induction. A narrative-biographical study on teacher socialisation. In: *Teaching and Teacher Education*, 18, pp. 105-120.

Kolodner, J. (1983): Towards an understanding of the role of experience in the evolution from novice to expert. In: *International Journal of Man-Machine Studies*, 19, pp. 497-518.

Kolodner, J. (1997): Educational implications of analogy: A view from case-based reasoning. In: *American Psychologist*, 52, pp. 57-66.

Minsky, M. (1994): Negative expertise. In: *International Journal of Expert Systems*, 7, pp. 9-13.

Oser, F./Spychiger, M. (2005): *Lernen ist schmerzhaft. Zur Theorie des negativen Wissens und zur Praxis der Fehlerkultur.* Weinheim: Beltz.

Parviainen, J./Eriksson, M. (2006): Negative knowledge, expertise and organisations. In: *International Journal of Management Concepts and Philosophy*, 2, pp. 140-153.

Patel, V. L./Ramoni, M.F. (1997): Cognitive models of directional inference in expert medical reasoning. In: Feltovich, P.J./Ford, K.M./Hoffman, R.R. (eds.): *Expertise in context: Human and machine.* Cambridge: AAAI/MIT Press, pp. 68-99.

Prenzel, M. (2010): Von der Unterrichtsforschung zur Exzellenz in der Lehrerbildung. In: *Beiträge zur Lehrerbildung*, 27, 3, pp. 327-345.

Rasch, B./Friese, M./Hofman, W./Naumann, E. (2006): *Quantitative Methoden. Band 2: Einführung in die Statistik.* Heidelberg: Springer.

Reason, J. (1990): *Human error.* Cambridge: Cambridge University Press.

Rybowiak, V./Garst, H./Frese, M./Batinic, B. (1999): Error Orientation Questionnaire (EOQ): Reliability, validity, and different language equivalence. In: *Journal of Organizational Behaviour*, 20, pp. 47-527.

Schank, R. (1999): *Dynamic memory revisited.* Cambridge: Cambridge University Press.

Strasser, J. (2006): *Erfahrung und Wissen in der Beratung.* Göttingen: Cuvillier.

van Woerkom, M. (2003): *Critical reflection at work. Bridging individual and organizational learning.* Twente: Twente University Press.

Watzke, J. (2007): Foreign language pedagogical knowledge: Toward a developmental theory of beginning teacher practices. In: *The Modern Language Journal*, 91, pp. 63-82.

Whyte, J./Ward, P./Eccles, D.W. (2009): The relationship between knowledge and clinical performance in novice and experienced critical care nurses. In: *Heart & Lung*, 38, pp. 517–525.

Wideen, M./Mayer-Smith, J./Moon, B. (1998): A critical analysis of the research on learning to teach: Making the case for an ecological perspective on inquiry. In: *Review of Educational Research*, 68, pp. 130-178.

6 Teachers' Knowledge about Domain Specific Student Errors

Janosch M. Türling, Jürgen Seifried and Eveline Wuttke

6.1 Professional Error Competence (PEC)

It is now commonly held that it is possible to develop professional competence by learning from errors at school and in the workplace (q.v. Baumgartner/Seifried in this edition). However, the idea that errors can bear a potential for learning was rarely supported at first (e.g. Weimer 1925). Recently, the focus has shifted to whether a negative evaluation of and response to errors is the most effective approach in pedagogical contexts (Fischer et al. 2006; Oser/Spychiger 2005; Yerushalmi/Pollingher 2006). A key aspect is seen in an 'error-friendly' learning environment. Here the teacher should both allay students' anxieties about making errors (emotional component) and enable reflection as well as support learning processes through feedback (cognitive component). Several disciplines study how teachers should best react to students' errors; namely, Pedagogy, Psychology, Medical Science, Neurology or Engineering Sciences (e.g. Bauer 2008; Graber 2009; Mehl/ Wehner 2008; Oser/Spychiger 2005; Weingardt 2004). Consequently, in the field of teaching-learning-research, increasing effort has been directed towards identifying error types and the possibility of learning from errors as well as analysing how teachers' behaviour influences students' chances of learning from errors (e.g. Baumert et al. 2010; Heinze 2004; Seidel/Prenzel 2007).

These questions can be dealt with against the background of the current discussion about teacher competences. Generally these are considered as distinctly different categories of professional knowledge, and three are seen as crucial: general pedagogical knowledge, pedagogical content knowledge and content knowledge (Graeber/Tirosh 2008; Hill/Ball/Schilling 2008; Shulman 1987). The broadest and most common definition of professional teacher competence portrays a complex construct which includes knowledge, beliefs and motivational orientations (Baumert/Kunter 2006; Desimone 2009). Referring to Shulman, pedagogical content knowledge (PCK) can be described as a specific type of knowledge on how to transform subject-matter knowledge into teaching practice. This kind of knowledge enables features such as the effective structuring of lessons, the use of specific representations or analogies, and an awareness of possible misconceptions or content-related learning difficulties (van Driel/Berry 2010). Despite rather broad research in this domain, it is still quite uncertain as to exactly what competences teachers should have in order to deal with errors constructively.

With this argument in mind, we suggest that in order to use students' errors constructively (from a cognitive point of view),[1] teachers need to be competent in three ways (three facets of Professional Error Competence, PEC):

1. *Knowledge of possible error types*: First, teachers have to actually recognise the specific logical flaws and false assumptions made by students. To be able to do this, teachers need domain-specific knowledge about possible learner errors.
2. *Available strategies of action/teacher reactions*: After having recognised the error, teachers must treat it 'adequately'. For this they have to know about various alternatives of action (e.g. providing adequate feedback or knowing when it is better to ignore errors).
3. *A constructive view on errors and their use in classroom interaction*: Roughly speaking, a so-called error-prevention-didactic (errors are to be prevented so that false trains of thought do not become habitual) can be set against a constructive management of errors. In the latter approach, teachers are prepared to become involved in students errors even if there are time constraints.

Our current project focuses on how teachers develop competence in the areas of error diagnosis and dealing with learner errors in the domain of accounting (Wuttke/Seifried 2009; Seifried/Wuttke 2010b). We assume that teachers can develop these competences in the course of their training and professional life. Because little is known about when teachers acquire error knowledge and ways of dealing with errors, we are using a combined cross-sectional longitudinal design to test teachers at several stages of their professional development. As a specific characteristic of the German teacher educational system, prospective teachers have to complete a Master's degree at university, where they already have didactical and pedagogical courses, and then successfully complete a practical training of about 1.5 to 2 years before they begin teaching. Therefore, corresponding development processes during professionalisation will be considered for four groups: bachelor's and master's students, pre-service teachers and professional teachers.

In this article we will focus on the first facet of PEC, namely the knowledge of possible error types. As our work is still in progress, the first findings concerning aspects of teachers' content knowledge (CK) will be discussed. This type of knowledge can be seen as a prerequisite for enabling teachers to diagnose typical student errors and handle these errors in an ade-

---

[1] For a more climatic or emotional point of view see also Spychiger et al. (1998) or Seifried/Wuttke (2010a).

quate way.[2] From a first view (cross-section of the above mentioned stages) the following objectives will be considered:

1. *What domain-specific knowledge about student errors do the participants have and are there differences due to the process of professionalisation?*
2. *How do they perceive their own knowledge and does this perception relate to actual performance?*

The following section of this chapter gives an overview of the theoretical foundation of learning from errors; in particular in the specific field of interest: accounting lessons in business education. How PEC could be measured and a description of our sample will be specified in chapter 6.3. Finally, empirical findings concerning knowledge and the ability to diagnose typical student errors (6.4) will be presented and discussed before the conclusion in section 6.5.

6.2 Student Errors in the Domain of Bookkeeping

6.2.1 Learning from Errors in School Settings

Analysing the process of learning from errors is difficult for both within domains and across domains, due to an unclear use of the term 'error' (Rohe/Beyer/Gerlach 2005: 15; Weingardt 2004: 199). Reasons could be found in a domain specific view as well as in linguistic barriers; in particular, many relevant research activities can be identified in English speaking countries. There, the use of terms like 'error', 'failure', 'fault', 'slip' or 'mistake' is not synonymous but rather conveys an intended differentiation (Senders/Moray 1991). For our research interests in the field of business education, and bookkeeping in particular, we refer to Heinze (2004: 223) who conceives student errors as domain specific and related to a specific setting of instruction. According to Heinze (2004) a situation in a classroom where errors occur is characterised by a triad of 1) a student's error, 2) 'public' error identification and 3) respective handling of students' errors by the teacher (225).

A possible basis for the modelling of error-learning-processes can be

---

2 As current research studies like COACTIV ("Cognitive Activation in the Classroom: Learning Opportunities for the Enhancement of Mindful Mathematics Learning", Baumert et al. 2010; Krauss et al. 2008) show, teachers' content knowledge can be seen as a necessary but not sufficient condition for the quality and effectiveness of teaching. So the PCK of a teacher (here to be aware of typical false assumptions of students, to have the ability to get to the bottom of student errors and to handle errors in an adequate way) apparently has a higher impact on the quality of teaching than the very existence of subject knowledge. Nevertheless, a substantial correlation between CK and PCK can be found.

found in the concept of negative knowledge or negative expertise. Recently Minsky (1994) popularised this concept (see also Oser/Spychiger 2005 or Gartmeier et al. 2008). Negative knowledge incorporates both procedural (knowledge, how something does not work; Minsky 1994) and declarative knowledge (knowledge, how something is not and what one does not know; Parviainen/Eriksson 2006). The basic idea is that people recognise their 'deficits' when they make mistakes and, as a consequence of this, initiate learning processes. Whether the potential connected with the acquisition of negative knowledge can actually develop and result in knowledge acquisition depends on whether deeper reasons for errors are analysed and reflected on, and whether constructive feedback is given on how to improve in the future. But the actual process of learning from errors, if it really happens, is still largely a mystery.[3] As a first step, a systematic conceptualisation of possible error types is necessary for every domain. A look beyond the border of our own discipline shows a long tradition of research in students' errors in subjects like language teaching (e.g. topics like 'fluency vs. accuracy') or mathematics (q.v. Seifried/Türling/Wuttke 2010). It is also remarkable that many student errors apparently neither occur randomly nor are they caused by a lack of concentration. Instead they can be recognised continuously and across generations (Swan 2004). Examples in language learning could be 'false friends' or in mathematics an incorrect use and exclusion of binomial phrases like $(a + b)^2 = a^2 + b^2$.

6.2.2 Domain Specific Considerations

Although the domain of bookkeeping can generally be seen as crucial for the development of economic competence (Preiß/Tramm 1996; Sembill/Seifried 2005; Sloane 1996), very little empirical evidence on its learning and instruction exists. Subsequently, we conducted a preliminary study interviewing experienced teachers (N = 51) about typical errors and error situations in the domain of bookkeeping. Accounting, in the opinion of (experienced) teachers and students, has a high rate of student errors. The results show that these errors can be classified using three different perspectives (Türling et al. in press).

---

[3] Even examinations at a physiological level do not paint a homogeneous picture. While, on the one hand, results point to the fact that errors have a positive effect on subsequent learning processes (Wills et al. 2007), on the other hand some people, because of an impaired processing of Dopamine, hardly seem to learn from the negative consequences of their actions (Klein et al. 2007).

1. *Subject topics that are prone to errors.* These are in particular: the transition from asset to profit & loss accounts, value added tax, adjusting entries and difficulties which refer to the logic and structure of this subject in general.
2. *Steps during a learning process*, which have to be paced within solving a task or a problem: the economic literacy, use of technical terms, formal operations like allocating to an account as well as constituting a booking record and mathematical operations.
3. *Possible causes for errors*: students' preconditions (e.g. cognitive abilities, a lack of interest), teachers' setting of priorities concerning content and methodological issues, teacher-caused errors, and the abstractness of the subject were most frequently mentioned.

Summarizing recent explanations of learning from errors and dealing with students' errors, these issues can be characterised as having both a high relevance and at the same time an insufficient evidence-base in the field of teaching-learning-research.

6.3 Method

6.3.1 Measurement of PEC

Current discussions and research trends concerning the assessment of competences are, among other things, characterised by a preference for behavioural data collected in performance situations, even if this means a higher test diagnostic effort than self-reports. However, a major disadvantage of using self-reports can be seen in the bias caused by over- or underestimation found in self-assessment (e.g. Leutner/Hartig/Jude 2008: 185f.). Simultaneously, to the increased impact of behavioural data, methodological progress, namely models of Item-Response-Theory (IRT), has enhanced the scope of new methods of test design and analysis (e.g. Adams/Wu 2002; Hartig 2009; van der Linden/Hambleton 1996; Walter 2005; Wu/Adams/Wilson/Haldane 2007). All in all, the current situation regarding the design and assessment of teacher competences still covers new territory and has not been sufficiently investigated using empirical evidence (e.g. Desimone 2009; Kunter/Baumert 2010).

For our purposes of measuring PEC, we refer to a mixed methods approach (Tashakkori/Teddlie 2008). Therefore, we use both performance data and self-reports to consider various areas of competence. To analyse the knowledge of (prospective) teachers about students' errors on the basis of performance data, we used video vignettes and a paper-pencil-test. The findings of the preliminary study (Interviews with experts, see chapter 6.2) formed the background for the production of the video vignettes. These vignettes present short error situations in the classroom and are used as prompts to test whether teachers are able to identify errors and how they respond (see also figure 1). The vignettes are interactive in such a way that a second sequence builds on the first. In the first sequence an error situation is shown to the participants. Afterwards, in a guided interview, the participants explain how they would react in the given situation, and especially how they would handle the error(s). Furthermore, it is recorded which errors the participants identify, and which causes they assume as reasons for the error(s). Depending on the participant's statement, one of four possible follow-up sequences is then activated. The test administrator has to choose one of them. The sequences vary systematically regarding two criteria: (1) The first aspect focuses on the extent to which the participants would give students hints for the correct solution and (2) the participants have to decide whether to take the entire class or single students into consideration by dealing with the shown problem/error. After the ending of the sequel the participants are again asked to explain their reaction in the shown situation. This multiple confrontation with a particular student error will show to what extent participants are able to present and explain an identical learning objective to students from different points of view. This ability is commonly seen as a reliable indicator for the pedagogical content knowledge and competence of a teacher (Brunner et al. 2006).

Using video vignettes to generate performance data has several advantages (e.g. Barter/Renold 1999; Jüttner/Neuhaus 2010; Oser/Salzmann/Heinzer 2009; Seguin/Ambrosio 2002; Veal 2002; Wason/Polonsky/Hyman 2002). Firstly, to measure PEC as an adequate and near to active treatment, a stimulus is needed that requests situative decisions on action – almost like in the 'real classroom'. In contrast to video-taping real classroom situations, the production of vignettes with professional actors ensures standardised conditions for the tests and the ability to vary and utilise typical errors that actually should be investigated. The one weakness of this instrument could be seen in social desirability, or that the vignettes in fact only represent a 'nearly realistic' situation.

In addition we used a paper-pencil-test to investigate knowledge about students' errors from another point of view. It was designed as a fictive class test including students' errors. The participants had to identify and correct these errors within a given time. Post-hoc analysis with item response modelling should present an appropriate way to assess how the participants scored in these performance tests and to ascertain the level of difficulty of the errors used. Here, due to the use of dichotomously scored responses such as 'correct' and 'incorrect' and constraints relating to sample size, a one-parameter logistic model (1PL, Rasch Model) was chosen (e.g. Hartig 2009; van der

Linden 2010). To obtain information on how the participants perceive their own knowledge about students' errors we used a standardized questionnaire (adapted version of a scale from the COACTIV-study). On a scale of 1 to 6 indicating their agreement with a statement like "I know in which tasks my students usually make errors." the participants mostly agreed (mean of about 4; 4 Items, Cronbach's α = .62).

Figure 1: Assessment of Competences with Video vignettes

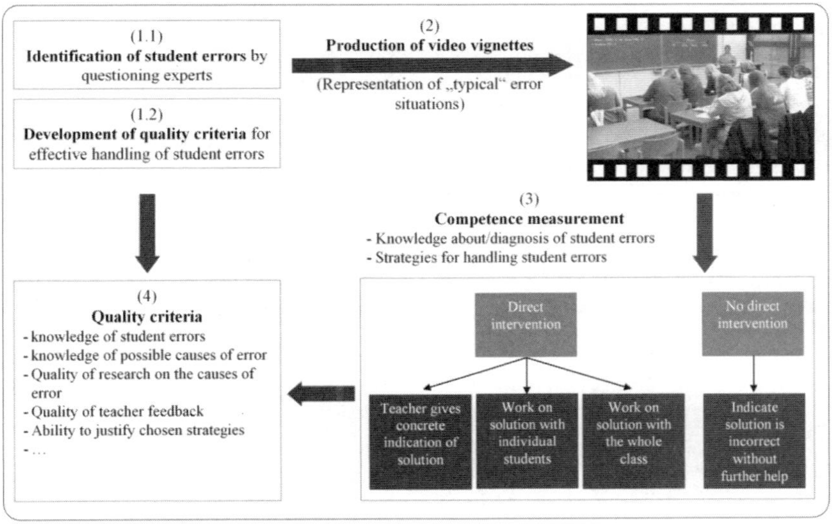

```
(1.1) Identification of student errors by questioning experts
(1.2) Development of quality criteria for effective handling of student errors
(2) Production of video vignettes (Representation of "typical" error situations)
(3) Competence measurement
 - Knowledge about/diagnosis of student errors
 - Strategies for handling student errors
(4) Quality criteria
 - knowledge of student errors
 - knowledge of possible causes of error
 - Quality of research on the causes of error
 - Quality of teacher feedback
 - Ability to justify chosen strategies
 - ...
Direct intervention:
 - Teacher gives concrete indication of solution
 - Work on solution with individual students
 - Work on solution with the whole class
No direct intervention:
 - Indicate solution is incorrect without further help
```

Source: own diagram

6.3.2 Sample

In 2010, data was collected from 285 German (prospective) teachers. The participants from stages 1 and 2 are in teacher training programmes at the Universities of Constance and Frankfurt. The pre-service teachers were attending their practical training at teacher education institutes, and the professional teachers were employed at commercial schools. All institutions considered are within the German federal states of Baden-Wuerttemberg and Hesse. At the time this paper was submitted, the completion of the sample was still in progress.

Table 1: Sample (n = 285)

Stage	N	sex		age		term/professional experience[4]	
		female	male	M	SD	M	SD
1-Teacher Training (Bachelor)	79	45	34	23.7	3.79	3.67	1.68
2-Teacher Training (Master)	78	53	25	26.8	4.87	2.28	1.03
3-Practical Training	74	32	42	28.9	3.77	.38	.26
4-Professional Teachers	54	33	21	32.8	4.56	3.77	1.81

Source: own table

With the exception of stage 3, gender distribution is slightly unbalanced in favour of female participants. The bachelor's students have an average age of about 24 and are in the middle of their undergraduate studies, the master's students are about 3 years older and are close to graduation. Participants from stage 3 are about 29 years old and are mostly at the beginning of their practical training, while the professional teachers have an average age of about 33 and an average of three and a half years teaching experience. The number of participants in the sample groups is slightly unbalanced because of 'panel mortality' and data sampling, as stage 4 is still incomplete.

6.4 Findings

6.4.1 Test Achievement and Comparison across Professionalization Steps

The subsequent figure 2 shows in detail how the participants (sorted by professionalization steps) scored in the tests (relative frequencies of correct item responses within their subgroup). To analyse possible differences between the four groups a chi-square test (df = 3) was used. The two vignette related tasks show that, apparently, the first task is easier to handle than the second task (all groups had correct responses of about 80 %), except for the professional teachers who scored high in both tasks. Thus, task V2 provides significant differences ($\chi^2 = 75.563$; p = .000). A look at the items related to the paper-pencil-test shows that the first task (PPT1) can be considered as being on a lower difficulty level with a statistical difference between groups ($\chi^2 = 14.138$; p = .003). The analysis of the other three items revealed that bachelor's and master's students, as well as pre-service teachers, achieved a rather

---

[4] Bachelor's and master's students = number of terms; pre-service and professional teachers = years of professional experience.

low score. Here the professional teachers once again scored (significantly) higher in the test (PPT2: $\chi^2 = 36.369$; PPT3: $\chi^2 = 19.117$; PPT4: $\chi^2 = 38.224$; p = .000 for all three items). All in all, with the exception of the two obviously easier tasks (V1 & PPT1), participants in the three earlier professionalisation steps did not differ substantially and achieved a rather low score, thus indicating that they did not recognise numerous errors. However, the professional teachers clearly outperformed the other groups. Comparing the average achievement of the four groups across all tasks showed significant differences and explained nearly 28 % of the variance (F = 36.851; p = .000; η^2 = .282). A linear increase of performance related to the different stages could not be found.

Figure 2: Chi-square Test: Correct item responses within subgroup (n = 285)

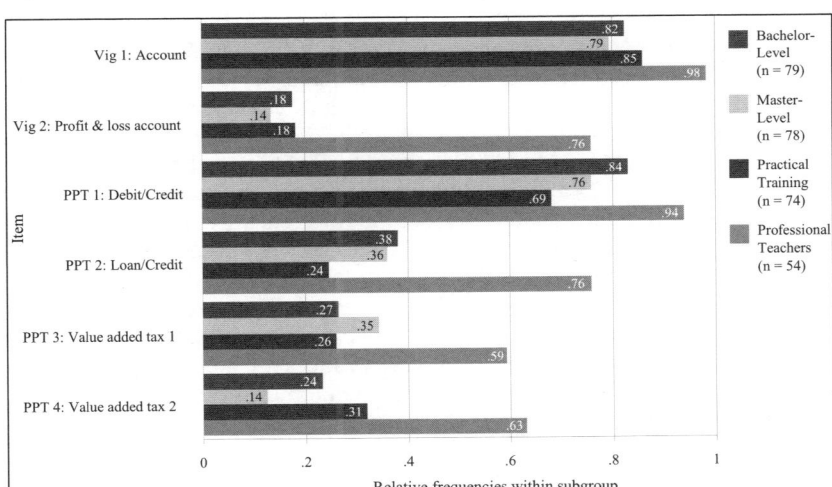

Source: own diagram

Whereas the above mentioned results were based on behavioural data, the self-perception of the participants regarding their ability to identify and correct errors will now be considered (Table 2). Altogether, the participants mostly perceive their own knowledge on a rather high level. A comparison of the four professionalisation steps showed significant differences (F = 13.126; p = .000) with a moderate effect size (explained variance η^2 = .123). Analysis of the relation between perception of knowledge and actual performance generates no significant correlation on group level. Looking at the aggregate level over all groups, only a low correlation (r = .16**) can be ascertained. Considering the test scores and a rather high level of agreement within the questionnaire, this is not surprising. However, the professional teachers apparently have both a higher ability (performance tests) and a more realistic self-perception (questionnaire).

Table 2: ANOVA: Self-perception of error diagnosis (n = 285)

Instrument	Stage	N	M	SD	F	P	η^2
Self report	1-Teacher Training (Bachelor's)	79	4.14	.55	13.126	.000	.123
	2-Teacher Training (Master's)	78	4.01	.60			
	3-Practical Training	74	3.82	.64			
	4-Professional Teachers	54	4.46	.49			

Note: Scale from 1 = full disagreement to 6 = full agreement. Cronbach's α = .62.

Source: own table

In order to test content knowledge or the ability to identify and correct domain-specific errors one has to include (domain-related) prior knowledge into analysis. A comparison of the mean values (test performance) due to socio-demographic variables of the bachelor's and master's students is given in Table 3. To avoid a possible bias, e.g. due to in-school practical experience of pre-service or professional teachers, only the students were taken into consideration. Here the school type, i.e. the different ways of achieving university entrance, and the students' practical experience were considered. The several types of business-related prior knowledge showed significant differences (F = 3.439; p = .018) but with a moderate effect size (explained variance η^2 = .063). Although prior knowledge is commonly held as a meaningful predictor for learning effectiveness, here the explained relation is rather low. This issue will be investigated more deeply in the ongoing research, e.g. by considering further variables and aspects.

Table 3: ANOVA: Prior knowledge of Bachelor's and Master's Students (n = 157)

Prior knowledge	N	M	SD	F	P	η^2
No prior knowledge	51	2.16	1.38			
Commercial secondary school	38	3.03	1.05	3.439	.018	.063
Dual vocational training	34	2.68	1.32			
Commercial sec. school & Dual vocational training	34	2.76	1.50			

Note: sum scores (range of 0 to 6)

Source: own table

6.4.2 Item-fit and IRT Parameters

Firstly, the Item-Fit must be proved. A 'good' Item-Fit and therefore a weighted MNSQ (weighted mean square) is commonly specified within a range of .75 to 1.33 (Adams/Khoo 1996; Bond/Fox 2001; quoted in Winther 2010: 152). Table 4 shows that all 6 items used in the performance tests are within the above mentioned range, and moreover, they mostly have an approximately exact fit (1.0). T-values have to be lower than 1.96 (at 5 % level of significance), which, in fact, applies for all 6 items. Furthermore, this post-hoc analysis of item-difficulties tends to ascertain two levels of difficulty (see also section 4.1). So the participants had to handle two rather easy tasks (V1 & PPT 1), and four more difficult tasks (V2, PPT 2, PPT 3 & PPT4).

Table 4: IRT - Item parameter estimates

Item[1]		Correct response (in %)	ESTIMATE	Weighted MNSQ	T	CI	Discriminatory Power
1	V1	84	-2.230	.98	-.10	(.78, 1.22)	.48
2	V2	28	1.343	.93	-1.0	(.86, 1.14)	.65
3	PPT1	79	-1.767	.97	-.30	(.82, 1.18)	.56
4	PPT2	41	.553	.99	-.10	(.88, 1.12)	.67
5	PPT3	34	.921	1.11	1.60	(.87, 1.13)	.55
6	PPT4	30	1.180	1.02	.30	(.86, 1.14)	.59

[1]Note: V = Vignette; PPT = Paper-pencil-test.
Separation Reliability = 0.996
Chi-square test of parameter equality = 878.12, df = 5, Sig. Level = .000

Source: own table

For the estimation of personal parameters the WLE (weighted likelihood) is commonly used and recommended (Hartig/Kühnbach 2006; Rost 2004; Wu 2005). Comparing item and personal parameters showed that the ability parameters are nearly equated to the sum score of the items.

A Wright map illustrating the estimates for the Rasch model is shown in Figure 3. The item difficulty and the personal ability are represented within the same dimension, meaning a response e.g. of item 2 indicates the highest level of ability, whereas, a response e.g. of item 3 indicates a lower level of ability. Although the additional use of an IRT-approach shows that the items fit well, because the set only has 6 items and the ability parameters are nearly equated to the sum score of the items (as mentioned above), the added value of this analysis here is low.

Figure 3: IRT (Wright map)

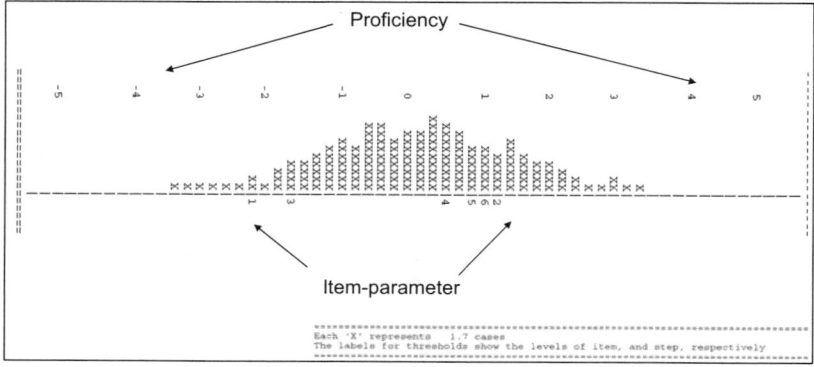

Source: own diagram

6.5 Conclusion

Coming back to the objectives presented in the beginning we can state:

1. *Knowledge about student errors*: the ability to identify and to correct errors (also in relation to the professionalisation step) of both students and pre-service teachers can, all in all, be seen as quiet low. Obviously school relevant content cannot be applied in an adequate way. This could be due to the fact that students quite often acquire inert knowledge which they are not able to use or apply in their professional life (Gruber/Renkl 2000). In contrast, the professional teachers scored very high in the tests, consequently generating significant differences. However, there is no linear positive relation between the stage of professionalisation and achievement in the tests.
2. *A comparison of self-perception and actual performance* showed low correlation. All in all students and pre-service teachers tend to overestimate their own ability to diagnose errors, whereas professional teachers apparently see their ability in a more realistic way (high perception and also high performance). According to section 3, this can be seen as a further argument for the use of performance data. Furthermore, a substantial relation (r = .50**) was generated by correlating the two single performance tests (video vignette and paper-pencil-test). For us, this is an indication that the two different

instruments measure similar competences, but do not provide exactly the same information. Thus, the vignettes could provide information which the paper-pencil-test did not.

However, due to the fact that the sample has not been completed yet, the findings should be seen as an initial tendency. As previously mentioned, this article only concerns the first facet of PEC: the diagnosis. In particular, only the ability to identify and to correct student errors, which is strongly related to content knowledge (CK), has been analysed. In ongoing research, further aspects of PEC and, in particular, the handling of errors by the teacher, such as getting to the bottom of an error cause or giving adequate feedback to enhance learning, will be analysed. Also the relation between single PEC-facets and further personality traits like self-regulation or self-efficacy must be taken into account.

References

Adams, R.J./Wu, M. (eds.) (2002): *PISA 2000 technical report*. Paris: OECD.

Barter, C./Renold, E. (1999): The use of vignettes in qualitative research. In: *Social Research Update 25*. Surrey: University of Surrey/Department of Sociology. Retrieved February 3, 2001, from http://sru.soc.surrey.ac.uk/SRU25.html.

Bauer, J.(2008): Fehler und Lernen aus Fehlern – Die Notwendigkeit deskriptiver und kumulativer empirischer Forschung. In: *Erwägen, Wissen, Ethik*, 19, pp. 306-310.

Baumert, J./Kunter, M./Blum, W./Brunner, M./Voss, T./ Jordan, A./Klusmann, U./ Krauss, S./Neubrand, M./Yi-Miau, T. (2010): Teachers' mathematical knowledge, cognitive activation in the classroom, and student progress. In: *American Educational Research Journal*, 47 (1), pp. 133-180.

Baumert, J./Kunter, M. (2006): Stichwort: Professionelle Kompetenz von Lehrkräften. In: *Zeitschrift für Erziehungswissenschaft*, 9, pp. 469-520.

Brunner, M./Kunter, M./Krauss, S./Klusmann, U./Baumert, J./ Blum, W./Neubrand, M./Dubberke, T./Jordan, A./Löwen, K./Yi-Miau, T. (2006): Die professionelle Kompetenz von Mathematiklehrkräften: Konzeptionalisierung, Erfassung und Bedeutung für den Unterricht. Eine Zwischenbilanz des COACTIV-Projekts. In: Prenzel, M./Allolio-Näcke, L. (eds.): *Untersuchungen zur Bildungsqualität von Schule. Abschlussbericht des DFG-Schwerpunktprogramms*. Münster et al.: Waxmann, pp. 54-82.

Desimone, L.M. (2009): Improving impact studies of teachers' professional development: Toward better conceptualizations and measures. In: *Educational Researcher*, 38, 3, pp. 181–199.

van Driel, J.H./Berry, A. (2010): The teacher education knowledge base: Pedagogical content knowledge. In: McGraw, B./Peterson, P.L./Baker, E. (eds.): *International Encyclopedia of Education*, 3rd edn., Oxford, UK: Elsevier, 7, pp. 656-661.

Fischer, M.A./Mazor, K.M./Baril, J./Alper, E./DeMarco, D./Pugnaire, M. (2006): Learning from mistakes. Factors that influence how students and residents learn from medical errors. In: *Journal of General Internal Medicine*, 21, 5, pp. 419–423.

Gartmeier, M./Bauer, J./Gruber, H./Heid, H. (2008): Negative knowledge: Understanding professional learning and expertise. In: *Vocations and Learning*, 1, pp. 87-103.

Graber, M.L. (2009): Educational strategies to reduce diagnostic error: can you teach this stuff? In: *Advances in Health Science Education*, 14, pp. 63-69.

Graeber, A.O./Tirosh, D. (2008): Pedagogical content knowledge: Useful concept or elusive notion. In: Sullivan, P./Woods, T. (eds.): *Knowledge and Beliefs in Mathematics Teaching and Teaching Development. The International Handbook of Mathematics Teacher Education.* Rotterdam: Sense Publisher, 1, pp. 117–132.

Gruber, H./Renkl, A. (2000): Die Kluft zwischen Wissen und Handeln: Das Problem des trägen Wissens. In: Neuweg, G.H. (ed.): *Wissen – Können – Reflexion.* Innsbruck et al.: Studien-Verlag, pp. 155-175.

Hartig, J. (2009): Messung der Kompetenzen von Lehrpersonen mit Modellen der Item-Response-Theorie. In: Zlatkin-Troitschanskaia, O./Beck, K./ Sembill, D./ Nickolaus, R./Mulder, R. (eds.): *Lehrerprofessionalität – Bedingungen, Genese, Wirkungen und Messung.* Weinheim: Beltz, pp. 295-310.

Hartig, J./Kühnbach, O. (2006): Estimating change using the plausible value technique within multidimensional Raschmodels. In: Ittel, A./Merkens, H. (eds.): *Veränderungsmessung und Längsschnittstudien in der empirischen Erziehungswissenschaft.* Wiesbaden: VS-Verlag, pp. 27-44.

Heinze, A. (2004): Zum Umgang mit Fehlern im Unterrichtsgespräch der Sekundarstufe I. Theoretische Grundlegung, Methode und Ergebnisse einer Videostudie. In: *Journal für Mathematik-Didaktik*, 25, pp. 221-245.

Hill, H.C./Ball, D.L./Schilling, S.G. (2008): Unpacking pedagogical content knowledge: Conceptualizing and measuring teachers' topic-specific knowledge of students. In: *Journal for Research in Mathematics Education*, 39, 4, pp. 372-400.

Jüttner, M./Neuhaus, B.J. (2010): Using empirically analyzed pupils' errors to develop a PCK test. In: Taşar, M.F./Çakmakci, G. (eds.): *Contemporary science education research: pre-service and in-service teacher education.* Ankara, Turkey: Pegem Akademi, pp. 331-340.

Klein, T./Neumann, J./Reuter, M./Hennig, J./von Cramon, Y.D. (2007): Genetically determined differences in learning from errors. In: *Science*, 318, 5856, pp. 1642-1645.

Krauss, S./Brunner, M./Kunter, M./Baumert, J./Blum, W./ Neubrand, M./Jordan, A. (2008): Pedagogical content knowledge and content knowledge of secondary mathematics teachers. In: *Journal of Educational Psychology*, 100, pp. 716-725.

Kunter, M./Baumert, J. (2010): Einführung in den Themenschwerpunkt „Lehrerforschung". In: *Unterrichtswissenschaft*, 1, pp. 3-4.

Leutner, D./Hartig, J./Jude, N. (2008): Measuring competencies: Introduction to concepts and questions of assessment in education. In: Hartig, J./Klieme, E./ Leutner, D. (eds.): *Assessment of Competencies in Educational Contexts.* Cambridge, MA: Hogrefe & Huber Publishers, pp. 177-192.

van der Linden, W.J. (2010): Item response theory In: McGraw, B./Peterson, P.L./Baker, E. (eds.): *International Encyclopedia of Education*, 3rd edn., Oxford, UK: Elsevier, 4, pp. 81-89.
van der Linden, W.J./Hambleton, R.K. (1996): *Handbook of modern item-response theory.* Berlin: Springer.
Mehl, K./Wehner, T. (2008). Über die Schwierigkeiten, aus Fehlern zu lernen. Auf der Suche nach einer angemessenen methodischen Vorgehensweise zur Untersuchung von Handlungsfehlern. In: *Erwägen, Wissen, Ethik*, 19, pp. 265-273.
Minsky, M. (1994): Negative expertise. In: *International Journal of Expert Systems*, 7, pp. 13-19.
Oser, F./Salzmann, P./Heinzer, S. (2009): Measuring the competence-quality of vocational teachers: An advocatory approach. In: *Empirical Research in Vocational Education and Training (ERVET)*, 1, 1, pp. 65-83.
Oser, F./Spychiger, M. (2005): *Lernen ist schmerzhaft. Zur Theorie des negativen Wissens und zur Praxis der Fehlerkultur.* Weinheim & Basel: Beltz.
Parviainen, J./Eriksson, M. (2006): Negative knowledge, expertise and organisations. In: *International Journal of Management Concepts and Philosophy*, 2, pp. 140-153.
Preiß, P./Tramm, T. (eds.) (1996): *Rechnungswesenunterricht und ökonomisches Denken.* Wiesbaden: Gabler.
Rohe, J./Beyer, M./Gerlach, F.M. (2005): Aspekte zu Risiken aus der Sicht der Health Professionals. In: Holzer, E./Hauke, E./Hochreuther, M.-A.(eds.): *Patientensicherheit – Leitfaden zum Umgang mit Risiken im Gesundheitswesen.* Wien, pp. 14-29.
Rost, J. (2004): *Lehrbuch Testtheorie – Testkonstruktion.* 2nd edn., Bern et al.: Huber.
Seidel, T./Prenzel, M. (2007): Wie Lehrpersonen Unterricht wahrnehmen und einschätzen – Erfassung pädagogisch-psychologischer Kompetenzen mit Videosequenzen. In: *Zeitschrift für Erziehungswissenschaft*, Sonderheft 8, pp. 201-216.
Seifried J./Türling, J.M./Wuttke, E. (2010): Professionelles Lehrerhandeln – Schülerfehler erkennen und für Lernprozesse nutzen. In: Warwas, J./Sembill, D. (eds.): *Schulleitung zwischen Effizienzkriterien und Sinnfragen.* Baltmannsweiler: Schneider Verlag Hohengehren, pp. 137-156.
Seifried, J./Wuttke, E. (2010a): Professionelle Fehlerkompetenz – Operationalisierung einer vernachlässigten Kompetenzfacette von (angehenden) Lehrkräften. In: *Wirtschaftspsychologie*, 12, 4, pp. 17-28.
Seifried, J./Wuttke, E. (2010b): Students' errors: how teachers diagnose them and how they respond to them. In: *Empirical Research in Vocational Education and Training (ERVET)*, 2 (2), pp. 5-21.
Seguin, C.A./Ambrosio, A.L. (2002): Multicultural vignettes for teacher preparation. In: *Multicultural Perspectives*, 4, pp. 10-16.
Sembill, D./Seifried, J. (eds.) (2005): *Rechnungswesenunterricht am Scheideweg. Lehren, lernen und prüfen.* Wiesbaden: Deutscher Universitäts-Verlag.
Senders, J.W./Moray, N.P. (1991): *Human error: cause, prediction and reduction.* New Jersey: Hillsdale.
Shulman, L.S. (1987): Knowledge and teaching: Foundations of the new reform. In: *Harvard Educational Research*, 57, pp. 1-22.
Sloane, P.F.E. (1996): *Didaktik des Rechnungswesens.* Pfaffenweiler: Centaurus-Verlagsgesellschaft.

Spychiger, M./Mahler, F./Hascher, T./Oser, F. (1998): *Fehlerkultur aus der Sicht von Schülerinnen und Schülern. Der Fragebogen S-UFS: Entwicklung und erste Ergebnisse. Schriftenreihe zum Projekt „Lernen Menschen aus Fehlern? Zur Entwicklung einer Fehlerkultur in der Schule", Nr. 4*. Pädagogisches Institut der Universität Fribourg, Schweiz.

Swan, M. (2004): Making sense of mathematics. In: Thompson, I. (ed.): *Enhancing primary mathematics teaching*, 2nd edn., Maidenhead: Open Univ. Press, pp. 111-124.

Tashakkori, A./Teddlie, C.B. (eds.) (2010): *Handbook of mixed methods in social and behavioural research,* 2nd ed., Thousands Oaks, London & New Delhi: Sage Publications.

Türling, J.M./Seifried, J./Wuttke, E./Gewiese, A./Kästner, R. (in press): ‚Typische' Schülerfehler im Rechnungswesenunterricht – Befunde einer Interviewstudie. In: *Zeitschrift für Berufs- und Wirtschaftspädagogik.*

Veal, W.R. (2002): Content specific vignettes as tools for research and training. In: *Electronic Journal of Science Education*, 6, 4, pp. 1-37.

Walter, O. (2005): *Kompetenzmessung in den PISA-Studien. Simulation zur Schätzung von Verteilungsparametern und Reliabilitäten.* Lengerich: Pabst.

Wason, K.D./Polonsky, M.J./Hyman, M.R. (2002): Designing vignette studies in marketing. In: *Austrailian Marketing Journal*, 10, pp. 41-58.

Weimer, H. (1925): *Psychologie der Fehler.* Leipzig: Klinkhardt.

Weingardt, M. (2004): *Fehler zeichnen uns aus. Transdisziplinäre Grundlagen zur Theorie und Produktivität des Fehlers in Schule und Arbeitswelt.* Bad Heilbrunn: Klinkhardt.

Wills, A.J./Lavric, A./Croft, G.S./Hodgson, T.L. (2007): Predictive learning, prediction errors, and attention. Evidence from event-related potentials and eye tracking. In: *Journal of Cognitive Neuroscience*, 19, 5, pp. 843–854.

Winther, E. (2010): *Kompetenzmessung in der beruflichen Bildung.* Bielefeld: Bertelsmann.

Wu, M.L. (2005): The role of plausible values in large-scale surveys. In: *Studies in Educational Evalutation*, 31, 2-3, pp. 114-128.

Wu, M.L./Adams, R.J./Wilson, M./Haldane, S.A. (2007): *ACER ConQuest. Version 2.0. Generalised Item Response Software.* Camberwell: ACER Press.

Wuttke, E./Seifried, J. (2009): Diagnose von und Umgang mit Schülerfehlern als Facette der professionellen Kompetenz von Lehrkräften – Skizze eines Forschungsprojekts. In: Wuttke, E./Ebner, H./Fürstenau, B./ Tenberg, R.(eds.): *Erträge und Perspektiven berufs- und wirtschaftspädagogischer Forschung. Schriftenreihe der Sektion Berufs- und Wirtschaftspädagogik der Deutschen Gesellschaft für Erziehungswissenschaft (DGfE).* Opladen & Farmington Hills: Barbara Budrich, pp. 45-54.

Yerushalmi, E./Pollingher, C. (2006): Guiding students to learn from mistakes. In: *Physics Education*, 41, pp. 532-538.

7 Errors, Emotions, and Learning in the Workplace – Findings from a Diary Study within VET

Andreas Rausch

7.1 Learning from Errors in the Workplace

On the one hand, errors in the workplace increase economic costs, create negative publicity, decrease customers' as well as employees' satisfaction (Zhao/Olivera 2006: 1012), and are, therefore, best avoided. On the other hand, it is argued that the costs of failing to learn from errors are far more widespread, yet much less studied (Detert/Edmondson 2006: 3). Errors remain a powerful means by which individuals in the workplace can learn. Within research conducted into emotion in the workplace, a similar turn became evident after rethinking lay beliefs that the best way to manage emotions in the workplace is not to have any (Elfenbein 2007: 316). Moreover, these strands of research are closely connected to learning. Errors typically cause negative emotional experience that, in turn, promotes changes in behaviour, i.e. learning.

7.1.1 Taxonomies of Human Error

Within action theory, action is defined as goal-oriented behaviour, while errors are seen as the avoidable non-attainment of a goal (Frese/Zapf 1994: 288; Zapf/Reason 1994: 427f.). Taxonomies of errors are typically defined on the basis of (I) the action phase and (II) the level of consciousness.

Ad (I): The proposed phases in the action process only differ in degrees of differentiation and denotations, dependent of the particular source, but, generally, bear the following structure: (1) Perception of the present situation and development of goals in terms of desired situations, (2) development of alternative plans (including omission), anticipation of effects, and assessment of one's own competence to implement a particular plan, (3) the decision, execution (overt behaviour), and monitoring of action, and (4) the processing of feedback in terms of analysing remaining discrepancies between the present and desired situation. In phase 1, *errors in goal setting* occur when goals are chosen or broken down into subgoals inadequately (Frese/Zapf 1994: 290). Within work environments, goals are usually given on a rather global unspecified level and need to be analysed further (Ellström 2001: 426f.). In phase 2, despite having the right goals in mind, plan development and judgment might be erroneous. Frese and Zapf (1994: 290), based on the work of Dörner, distinguish between errors in information gathering, interpretation, and elaboration (*mapping errors*), *prognosis errors* with regard to future developments of a situation, and *thought errors*, which refer in particular to the disregard of side and long-term effects. *Memory errors* occur in the monitoring of action when plans or subplans are simply forgotten. *Judgment errors* refer to the overlooking or misinterpretation of feedback.

Ad (II): Action theory approaches distinguish between levels of consciousness in which the phases of action are processed (Hacker 1978: 105; Rasmussen 1983: 258; Leventhal/Scherer 1987: 17; Eraut 2000: 129). One basic assumption is that conscious processes are expensive in terms of energy consumption and slow because of the limited capacity of conscious information processing (Dörner/Schaub 1994: 447). Well-known automated routines, therefore, are assigned to lower levels of consciousness, while conscious processing allows for problem solving, i.e. the handling of situations, in which successful routines are not (yet) available (Dörner/Wearing 1995). The latter demands a steady and expensive investment of awareness (Heckhausen/Beckmann 1990: 38). According to common classifications, errors within conscious processing are defined as *mistakes*, indicating either a failure of available expertise or a lack of expertise (Reason 1990: 12f). These kinds of errors—also referred to as *knowledge errors*—appear more frequently in novices (Frese/Zapf 1994: 291). In contrast to mistakes on a conscious level, *slips* and *lapses* occur in particular within unconscious routines of action. They indicate errors of storage (lapses) or execution (slips) (Reason 1990: 13) and are best characterised by a short-term lack of concentration or absentmindedness (Heckhausen/Beckmann 1990: 39). These errors are likely to occur in monotonous work tasks that are subjectively perceived as boring and uninteresting (Loukidou et al. 2009: 384). The experience of monotony, which corresponds to below capacity consumption of conscious processing, presumes that the task at hand is already well known, easy to learn, or rather, not challenging. Therefore, it is argued that slips and lapses occur within tasks that individuals are experts in (Frese/Altmann 1989: 69f).

7.1.2 Feedback, Emotion, and Socio-cultural Aspects in Learning from Errors

With regard to learning from errors, feedback of any kind is a necessary condition for detecting errors (Frese/Zapf 1994: 291), which, in turn, is a necessary condition for learning from errors. Goal progression might be directly assessable because of the particular task characteristics or indirectly assessable by means of *augmented* or *quickened feedback*, which is implemented on purpose (acoustic signals in machines, error messages in software applications etc.) (Hacker/Skell 1993: 166; Frese/Zapf 1994: 279). For novices, a third kind of feedback, i.e. feedback from significant external agents such as colleagues, trainers, supervisors, and customers, is of particular importance. If this communicative feedback is enriched with information about why a particular error occurred, which goals were missed, and what could be improved, it becomes a fruitful source of learning (Ilgen et al. 1979: 350f; see also Seifried/Baumgartner, this volume).

The bottom line of feedback processing, from whatever source it may arise, is the individual's interpretation of it. Aside from intentional workplace sabotage, errors usually go hand in hand with negative emotions. In fact, given an error is detected, it would challenge the very definition of error, if there were no consequences at the emotional level, because one could question if there were any goal directing the action at all.

Results from an exploratory study on organisational events and resulting emotions among 101 hotel employees show that task problems, lack of goal achievement, and making mistakes lead to varying negative emotions such as embarrassment, worry, disappointment, unhappiness, and fear, whereas goal progress, problem-solving, and goal achievement lead to positive emotions such as pleasure, relief, happiness, pride, etc. (Basch/Fisher 2000: 43ff). By means of a diary study, Harris et al. (2003) show that goal-attainment in the course of a day leads to enhanced well-being and activated affective states by the end of that day. This relationship turns out even stronger the more personally important goals are. These appraisal mechanisms provide a natural basis for learning, because humans strive for the retention of positive emotion and the prevention of negative emotion (Sembill 1992; Scherer 1994: 130). Negative emotions linked to present errors signal a need for reflection on, and modification of, the apparently ineffective action approaches. Memories of negative emotions linked to past errors prevent us from committing the same error again (Oser 2007: 204). Nevertheless, relying solely on the deterrent effects of errors is not deemed to be a favourable condition for learning. A constant fear of making errors, especially on the part of novices, prevents them from meeting new challenges and, hence, reduces learning chances as well. According to the self-determination theory of motivation (Deci/Ryan 1985), errors impair the basic psychological need for experiencing one's own competence. Furthermore, whenever errors become observable to external agents, especially colleagues and supervisors, the basic need for social relatedness may also be impaired as well as the need for autonomy, as responsibility and scope might be reduced. A more positive learning culture must not 'glorify' errors, but handle them in such a way that allows learning from them (Oser 2007: 203ff). In such a workplace culture, people do ask for help, admit errors, and discuss problems, instead of merely concealing errors or attributing blame (Edmondson 1999: 352; Harteis et al. 2008: 225). From two studies with more than 100 organisations, Dyck et al.

(2005) results report positive correlations between the extent of an *organisational error management culture* (i.e. communicating about, detecting, analysing, and correcting errors) and several organisational performance measures. Similarly, findings from a mixed-method study by Edmondson (1999) support the hypothesis that *psychological safety* supports team learning, which in turn affects team performance. Arenas et al. (2006) found that participants focused in learning goal orientation, in contrast to those pursuing performance goals, processed feedback more constructively and, therefore, learned from their errors and showed higher performance in the long run. In discussing the results, the authors suggest that learning goal orientation can be fostered through a balanced design of results in the short- and long-term, when the potential for improvement is identified and cooperation among coworkers is fostered (ibid.: 583), referring to socio-cultural influences. Thus, an individual's handling of errors—as for instance measured by the error orientation questionnaire (Rybowiak et al. 1999)—can be interpreted as an expression of the culture of learning from errors in the particular organisation (Harteis et al. 2008). Error handling, emotional experience, and learning in the workplace, as in human behaviour in general, are dependent on individual *and* environmental factors that, in turn, interact with each other.

7.1.3 Hypotheses

Despite of the rather exploratory character of the study, based on the above discussion, the following hypotheses are proposed:

- H1a: Error occurrence is positively correlated with perceived novelty and difficulty of a task.
- H1b: Error occurrence is positively correlated with received feedback from colleagues.
- H2: Errors are positively correlated with the extent of perceived learning.
- H3: Errors are positively correlated with negative emotional states.

Further exploratory analysis is presented in the respective result sections.

7.2 Data and Method

7.2.1 Participant Characteristics

The study was conducted in the field of vocational education and training

(VET) in Germany and focused on the informal learning processes in the workplace. All participants were trainees at differing stages of a three-year apprenticeship programme to become *industrial clerks* (German: "*Industriekaufmann/-frau*") employed by an automotive subcontractor company.[1] The sample of 21 trainees (14 females, 7 males) had an average age of 20 years, ranging from 17 to 24. During their workplace periods, trainees are assigned to different departments (marketing, controlling, customer service etc.), each for several weeks. They are introduced to the work of the department by skilled workers and perform work tasks increasingly without further assistance. While those skilled workers are experts in the domain of the particular department, they are not typically educated as trainers.

7.2.2 Procedure and Measures

The study extended from May to August 2010. The study design involved standardised questionnaires administered twice at an interval of about four weeks. Within this period, participants were asked to keep an Internet-based work diary for at least ten workdays. The diary period was set individually for each trainee with regard to department changes, vacations, and vocational school periods. For the purpose of this paper and due to limited space, only some of the collected data is analysed here.

Error orientation. The original error orientation questionnaire (EOQ) by Rybowiak et al. (1999) consists of 37 items in eight dimensions. By means of factor-analysis in a German version of the EOQ, Bauer et al. (2003) found three dimensions that included 20 items. However, in the sample at hand, two more items were excluded to improve item-scale consistency (Cronbach's alpha). Table 1 shows the psychometric properties as well as a sample item of the three scales in use.

---

[1] My thanks go to Caroline Weinig who was of great help throughout the study.

Table 1: Means, standard deviation, intercorrelations, and internal consistencies (in parentheses) of the error orientation scales

Scale	Sample item	M	SD	1	2	3
1. Positive appraisal of errors (8 items)	Errors assist me to improve my work.	5.18	.80	(.75)		
2. Strategies to learn from errors (4 items)	After I have made an error, I think about how it came about.	5.68	.83	.48*	(.74)	
3. Negative emotions regarding errors (6 items)	I am often afraid of making errors.	3.00	.99	-.09	.33	(.82)

Note. n = 21. * p < .05 (two-tailed). Correlations calculated using Pearson's r. Tested for normality using the Kolmogorov-Smirnov test. Internal consistencies (Cronbach's alspha) are presented in parentheses along the diagonal indicating satisfying scale values. Items were rated on a 7-point Likert scale from 1 (totally disagree) to 7 (totally agree). Items were retranslated from the German version of the EOQ (Bauer et al. 2003) by the author.

Source: own table

Basic need satisfaction. According to self-determination theory (Deci/Ryan 1985) the basic needs for autonomy, competence, and social relatedness are crucial for well-being, the development of intrinsic motivation, and psychological growth, i.e. personality development and learning. Basic need satisfaction was measured in both measurement points (MP1, MP2) using a prevalent German questionnaire by Prenzel (1994). Table 2 presents the psychometric statistics as well as a sample item of the three scales.

Table 2: Means, standard deviation, and internal consistencies of the basic need satisfaction scales in MP1 and MP2

Scale	Sample item	Measurement point 1			Measurement point 2		
		M	SD	CA	M	SD	CA
Autonomy	I take responsibility for challenging tasks.	3.80	.83	.82	3.72	.83	.77
Competence	Complex tasks are assigned to me.	3.88	.86	.82	3.48	.94	.87
Relatedness	I feel understood and supported.	4.48	1.10	.95	4.50	1.16	.95

Note. n = 21. Internal consistencies are calculated using Cronbach's alpha (CA) indicating satisfying scale values. Items were rated on a 6-point Likert scale from 1 (totally disagree) to 6 (totally agree). Items were retranslated from the German version of the motivation questionnaire (Prenzel 1994) by the author.

Source: own table

Work diary: Based on similar approaches by Noss and Achtenhagen (2002) and Rausch (2011), insight into work processes was gained by using work diaries. Diary-methods try to overcome memory biases by collecting data near real-time or, at least, with far shorter time delays than common retrospective instruments. Thus, diaries offer a means of analysing fluctuating data collected within participants' natural environments (for overviews, see Laireiter et al. 1997, Bolger et al. 2003, Brandstätter 2007, Ohly et al. 2010). There are no diary studies researching errors, emotion, and learning in the workplace known to the author.

In the present study, the work diary was implemented as a Flash®-based Internet-application.[2] The participants were asked to record about five tasks per day over a period of ten workdays. The tasks recorded were to be randomly chosen, and to be typical of the respective days. Each task record included four steps: First, the participant had to assign the task at hand to one of nine predetermined formal task types including *miscellaneous*. In the second step, for each task, trainees were asked for a short verbal description and to enter the duration of the task. Next, the participants had to complete ten standardised items referring to characteristics of the task at hand, among others, including the *novelty* and *difficulty*, the degree of *errors* made during the task, the extent of received *feedback* from colleagues, and the perceived *learning* from the task. All items were presented as a 6-point Likert scale from 1 (*lowest degree*) to 6 (*highest degree*). In a final step, the trainees were asked to record up to three different emotional states they experienced throughout the task. These items were arranged according to common circumplex models of emotion—the x-axis showing valence, the y-axis showing arousal. Figure 1 shows a screenshot taken from the Internet-based diary. For information on the coding of answers see figure notes. To avoid redundant information, descriptive statistics are presented in the results section.

---

2   My thanks go to Frank Reinhardt, who skilfully developed the application within a project seminar according to the requested specifications.

Figure 1: Screenshot of the instrument for measuring emotional states within the Internet-based work diary

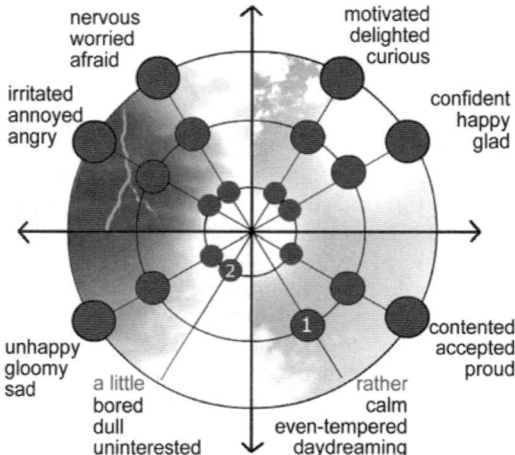

Note. Participants could comment on their emotional state during the task by mouse-clicking on up to three of the spots. The intensity of the emotional state could vary from *a little* (smaller spot near the centre, coded as 1) to *very* (bigger outer spots, coded as 3). Emotional states that were not chosen were coded with 0. In the above screenshot, a participant reports having felt *rather calm/even-tempered/day–dreaming* and also *a little bored/dull/uninterested*. The numbers displayed in the spots indicate the sequence of selection made by the participants, not the coded value. English translation by the author.

Source: own diagram

7.2.3 Sample Sizes

Participant flow, sample sizes. While all 21 participants completed the standard questionnaires in MP1 and MP2, participation in the diary period varied. As analysis on the person-level demanded the calculation of an average perception of task characteristics and emotional states for each participant – for those analyses, a minimum of task records from each participant was required. Therefore, five participants were excluded because they recorded fewer than 20 tasks. The remaining sample of 16 trainees recorded 787 tasks in total, amounting to an average of 49.2 tasks each, varying from 21 up to 91. However, those analyses restricted to the task-level were based on a sample of 573 tasks including only work tasks. Tasks assigned to other formal task types were excluded.

Missing data. While there is no missing data in the questionnaire data set on an individual level, there is some missing data in the data set of tasks. Missing data is treated by pairwise deletion. There is no data imputation applied, because data is missing due to plausible reasons, whenever a certain task characteristic item was not appropriate for a particular task. Accordingly, sample sizes vary due to missing data.

7.3 Results

Alpha-level and effect sizes. Reported p values are two-tailed with an alpha level of .05 indicating statistical significance. P values less than .05 are marked with one asterisk; p values less than .01 are marked with two asterisks. Correlation coefficients between .20 and .40 indicate small effect sizes, those between .40 and .60 indicate medium effect sizes, and correlation coefficients higher than .60 are considered as large effect sizes. Furthermore, eta-squares (η^2) are calculated as measures of explained variance in tests of mean differences, with $\eta^2 > .01$ indicating small effects, $\eta^2 > .06$ indicating medium effects, and $\eta^2 > .14$ indicating large effects.

7.3.1 Error Occurrence and Learning from Errors

In order to gain initial insights into error occurrence, the distribution of the task item *errors* is first regarded. This item was answered in 525 work tasks, in 48 cases the item remained blank. In the present sample, the participating trainees, in general, reported low degrees of errors (Mean = 1.39, Median = 1, Mode = 1, SD = .725). For 376 work tasks, trainees reported having made no error at all (scale value 1 = 71.6 %), whereas scale value 6 (*many and/or major errors*) was not selected at all. Between these poles, errors to varying degrees were reported in 149 work tasks. The distribution is heavily right-skewed (skewness index = 2.08). This finding is not surprising since small slips and lapses, which are immediately detected and corrected on one's own, might not be recognised as errors at all, indicating a narrower understanding of the term error on the part of the trainees. Grouped by formal task types, *profession-specific communication with externals*, such as customers, suppliers etc. turned out to be the most prone to errors.

H1a and H1b: Error occurrence, novelty, difficulty, and feedback from colleagues. Since data was not normally distributed (KS test), the Spearman rank order correlation coefficients were calculated. Results confirmed the hypothesised correlations between *error occurrence* and (i) *novelty* of a task (r = .21**, p = .000, n = 525 tasks), (ii) *difficulty* of a task (r = .51**, p =

.000, n = 522), and (iii) *feedback* from colleagues within a task (r = .29**, p = .000, n = 510). The correlation between *difficulty* and *errors* showed a medium effect size, whereas the other two showed only small effect sizes.

H2: errors and learning. As hypothesised, the task items *errors* and *learning* were positively correlated (Spearman's r = .412**, p < .001, n = 516). Furthermore, the correlation between errors and learning was also found on a person-level. For this purpose, task items were aggregated for each participant presenting an average occurrence of errors with respect to an average perception of learning in the course of the diary period. The analysis on the person-level revealed a large correlation between the average reporting of errors and the average perception of having learned something from work tasks (Spearman's r = .60*, p = .014, n = 16).

7.3.2 Errors and Related Emotional States

H3: Errors and emotional states. In order to address hypothesis H3b, the correlation between the degrees of errors within a task and the emotional states related to the particular task were analysed. Table 3 shows descriptive statistics and the results of the analysis.

Table 3: Correlations between degrees of errors and emotional states on task-level

Emotional states	Descriptive statistics		Correlation analysis	
	M	SD	r	p
1. motivated / delighted / curious	.71	.96	.02	.70
2. confident / happy / glad	1.10	1.01	-.15**	.00
3. contented / accepted / proud	.96	1.11	.01	.83
4. calm / even-tempered / daydreaming	1.08	1.25	.10*	.02
5. bored / dull / uninterested	.53	1.03	-.09*	.04
6. unhappy / gloomy / sad	.12	.55	.17**	.00
7. irritated / annoyed / angry	.13	.59	.02	.59
8. nervous / worried / afraid	.23	.73	.34**	.00

Note. n = 525 work tasks. Since data were not normally distributed (KS test), the Spearman rank order correlation coefficients are calculated.

Source: own table

First of all, the mean values of emotional states appear very low, but this is not surprising, since participants could only rate a maximum of three of the eight presented emotional states. Thus, whenever a particular emotional state was not rated, the item value was set to zero. The mean values indicate that, on average, the trainees experienced more positive (items 1 to 4) than negative (items 5 to 8) emotional states within work tasks, whereas the proportion of rather activated (items 1, 2, 7, 8) to rather inactive states is more balanced.

With regard to hypothesis H2, five of eight correlations are statistically significant. All of them show the expected trends, supporting the hypothesis, except for *calm / even-tempered / daydreaming*. Only *nervous / worried / afraid* shows a noticeable effect size. Similar results were obtained by a Mann-Whitney-U test for differences on the dichotomised variable *error* (group 1 = tasks with no errors at all, n = 376; group 2 = tasks with errors of varying degrees, n = 149). Significant mean differences were observed for *confident / happy / glad* (lower mean value in group 2, p = .001, η^2 = .016), *calm / even-tempered / daydreaming* (higher mean value in group 2, p = .017, η^2 = .015), *unhappy / gloomy / sad* (higher mean value in group 2, p = .001, η^2 = .012), and *nervous / worried / afraid* (higher mean value in group 2, p < .001, η^2 = .062). Again, only *nervous / worried / afraid* showed a medium effect size. Altogether, errors in the workplace do go along with rather negative emotional states, thus giving support to the hypothesis, with the exception of *calm / even-tempered / daydreaming* states.

Surprisingly, the correlations between errors and emotional states revealed a completely different picture when analysed on the person-level. For this purpose, task data was aggregated for each participant representing an average occurrence of errors and an average experience of emotional states. The aggregated means for each participant was weighted by task duration. Table 4 shows descriptive data and the results of the correlation analysis.

Table 4: Degrees of errors and emotional states on person-level

Emotional states	Descriptive statistics		Correlation analysis	
	M	SD	r	p
1. motivated / delighted / curious	1.14	.30	.69**	.00
2. confident / happy / glad	.49	.38	.53*	.04
3. contented / accepted / proud	.75	.51	.68**	.00
4. calm / even-tempered / daydreaming	.64	.53	.61*	.01
5. bored / dull / uninterested	.73	.58	.64**	.01
6. unhappy / gloomy / sad	.45	.38	.17	.53
7. irritated / annoyed / angry	.09	.19	-.15	.59
8. nervous / worried / afraid	.12	.15	.37	.16

Note. n = 16 trainees. Diary data was aggregated to person-level by calculating means of the task-item error and emotional states for each individual. Since data were not normally distributed (KS test), the Spearman rank order correlation coefficients are calculated.

Source: own table

Contrary to the findings on task-level, there were high correlations between errors and positive emotional states on the person-level. This means that, the more trainees reported errors in the course of the diary period, the more positive their average emotional experience was. This is surprising because, within a concrete task, errors go hand in hand with negative emotional states (see table 3).

Further exploratory analysis regarding socio-cultural aspects revealed a plausible explanation for these ostensibly contradictory findings. Though the mean values of basic need satisfaction shown in table 2 did not differ much between MP1 and MP2, this does not indicate that the changes for each participant did not differ either. Correlation analysis was conducted between errors on the one hand and changes of basic need satisfaction from MP1 to MP2 (delta = value$_{MP2}$ - value$_{MP1}$) on the other hand. The underlying question is: To what extent are errors made in the course of the diary period related to changes in basic need satisfaction? There are significant correlations between *errors* and *experienced autonomy* (Pearson's r = .60*, p = .01, n = 16) and *experienced social relatedness* (Pearson's r = .53*, p = .03, n = 16). Though errors are not correlated with *experienced competence* (Pearson's r = .09, p = .75, n = 16), the other two correlations are, in my opinion, extraordinary in that there is no *common method bias* at all. The presented relations might be an expression of a particular learning-conducive atmosphere within apprenticeships. Indeed, compared to findings from a study with experienced employees (Bauer et al. 2003: 19), the means of error orientation (see section procedure and measures) showed a notable difference. While the first two scales—*positive appraisals of errors* and *strategies to learn from errors*—showed similar means, the mean of the scale *negative emotions regarding errors* turned out to be noticeably lower—3.00 in the sample at hand compared to 5.35 and 5.14 as found by Bauer and colleagues. Apparently, trainees are less afraid of making errors, a finding that, in turn, argues for a positive culture of learning from errors. Further discussion will follow in the final section.

7.4 Discussion

The first research question underlying the analyses addressed error occurrence. Though the measurement of errors—especially that of small errors—within daily work is supposed to be challenging (Rasmussen 1982: 314), errors of varying degrees were reported for 149 out of 573 work tasks. Thus, the diary method seems to be an appropriate empirical approach. Nevertheless, one has to assume that, the more errors take the form of nearly unconscious slips and lapses (which are immediately detected and corrected), the less they are reported in the work diary. As hypothesised and in line with common sense, error occurrence corresponds to the novelty and, in particular, the difficulty of a task. Furthermore, error occurrence is correlated with feedback from colleagues. As already discussed in the theory section, feedback seems to be a powerful source of error detection, especially for novices. With regard to learning from errors, significant correlations between reported errors and perceived learning were found on both the task-level and person-level, indicating that errors are an important source of learning for trainees.

Another field of interest concentrated on the relation between errors and emotional state. In the present sample, errors were likely to accompany higher ratings in negative emotional states, in particular, being *nervous / worried / afraid*. An exception was the rather inactive and yet positive emotional state of being *calm / even-tempered / daydreaming* showing a positive correlation with error occurrence, too, but of only small effect size. As the applied measurement of errors and emotional states does not allow for causal interpretations, it seems reasonable to assume that feeling nervous, worried, or afraid is a consequence of errors, whereas calm, even-tempered, and daydreaming moods might rather be antecedents to errors in terms of slips and lapses caused by absentmindedness.

Surprisingly, further analysis on the person-level, i.e. analysis on aggregated process data for each participant, showed a different picture. On average, trainees reporting more errors in the course of the diary period reported more positive emotional states, although, as stated above, the very occurrence of an error goes along with rather negative emotions. Results from exploratory analyses give a (to my mind) convincing explanation. Firstly, with regard to socio-cultural aspects of learning from errors, trainees in the present sample showed noticeably low scores on the scale *negative emotions regarding errors* taken from the error orientation questionnaire adapted by Bauer et al. (2003). This can be seen as an indicator of a positive culture of learning from errors. Furthermore, aggregated error occurrence showed significant positive correlations with the changes in basic need satisfaction (*experienced autonomy* and *experienced social relatedness*) from measurement point 1 to measurement point 2. This means that, the more trainees reported errors within the diary period, the more their basic need satisfaction increased. It seems, as a result of the positive learning culture, that making errors does not lead to deprivation of autonomy or social exclusion, but instead leads to increased help and feedback from others (see analysis on task-level), which in turn leads to higher social support and, thus, more positive emotional states. In summary, errors in the workplace cause negative emotions in the short term, but in the long term they might lead to positive emotions. This correlation is mediated by basic need satisfaction and moderated by a positive culture of learning from errors. Admittedly, the assumptions do not explain the positive correlation between errors and the experience of *bored / dull / uninterested* states shown in table 4. Moreover, the latter assumptions are derived from exploratory analysis and are not meant to be hard and fast, but instead require further research.

Considering the large heterogeneity of work environments, the results of this study require replication. Regarding research designs, the findings suggest that, when exploring learning from errors in the workplace, emotional states should be taken into account. Closely connected to this suggestion is a methodological one. It seems worthwhile to collect data as close to the processes as possible, instead of relying solely on retrospective reports by means of questionnaires or interviews. The Internet-based work diary applied in the present study served this purpose very well. Nevertheless, there are limitations to this method regarding the amount of information gathered for each task as well as the confirmation of causality. In future research, additional interviews focusing on diary entries of particular interest might help to get a still closer insight, provided those interviews are also conducted as promptly as possible after the entry.

References

Arenas, A./Tabernero, C./Briones, E. (2006): Effects of goal orientation, error orientation and self-efficacy on performance in an uncertain situation. In: *Social Behavior and Personality*, 34, 5, pp. 569-586.
Basch, J./Fisher, C. (2000): Affective events-emotions matrix: A classification of work events and associated emotions. In: Ashkanasy, N./ Härtel, C./Zerbe, W. (eds.): *Emotions in the Workplace: Research, Theory, and Practice*. Westport Connecticut, London: Quorum Books, pp. 36-48.
Bauer, J./Festner, D./Harteis, C./Gruber, H. (2003): *Fehlerorientierung im betrieblichen Arbeitsalltag. Ein Vergleich zwischen Führungskräften und Beschäftigten ohne Führungsfunktion*. Research Report, University of Regensburg. Retrieved April 4, 2011, from http://www-campus.uni-r.de/gruber/images/stories/ PDF/Forschungsberichte/ fb05.pdf.
Bolger, N./Davis, A./Rafaeli, E. (2003): Diary methods: Capturing life as it is lived. In: *Annual Review of Psychology*, 54, 1, pp. 579-616.
Brandstätter, H. (2007): The time sampling diary (TSD) of emotional experience in everyday life situations. In: Coan, J.A./Allen, J.J.B. (eds.): *Handbook of Emotion Elicitation and Assessment*. Oxford: Oxford University Press, pp. 318-331.
Deci, E.L./Ryan, R.M. (1985): *Intrinsic motivation and self-determination in human behavior*. New York: Plenum Press.
Detert, J.R./Edmondson, A.C. (2006): *Everyday failures in organizational learning: Explaining the high threshold for speaking up at work*. Manuscript, Harvard Business School. Retrieved April 4, 2001, from http://www.hbs.edu/units/tom/ docs/detert-edmond-son.pdf.
Dörner, D./Wearing, A.J. (1995): Complex problem solving: Toward a (computer-simulated) theory. In: Frensch, P.A./Funke, J. (eds.): *Complex Problem Solving – The European Perspective*. Hillsdale: Lawrence Erlbaum, pp. 65-99.
Dörner, D./Schaub, H. (1994): Errors in planning and decision-making and the nature of human information processing. In: *Applied Psychology: An International Review*, 43, 4, pp. 433-453.
Edmondson, A. (1999): Psychological safety and learning behavior in work teams. In: *Administrative Science Quarterly*, 44, pp. 350-383.

Elfenbein, H.A. (2007): Emotion in organizations. A review and theoretical integration. In: *The Academy of Management Annals*, 1, pp. 315-386.
Ellström, P.-E. (2001): Integrating learning and work: Problems and prospects. In: *Human Resource Development Quarterly*, 12, 4, pp. 421-435.
Eraut, M. (2000): Non-formal learning and tacit knowledge in professional work. In: *British Journal of Educational Psychology*, 70, pp. 113-136.
Frese, M./Altmann, A. (1989): The Treatment of errors in learning and training. In: Bainbridge, L./Quintanilla, S.A.R. (eds.): *Developing Skills with New Technology*. Chichester: Wiley, pp. 65-86.
Frese, M./Zapf, D. (1994): Action as the core of work psychology: A German approach. In: Triandis, H.C./Dunnette, M.D./Hough, L.M. (eds.): *Handbook of Industrial and Organizational Psychology*, Vol. 4. Palo Alto: Consulting Psychologists Press, pp. 271-340.
Hacker, W. (1978): *Allgemeine Arbeits- und Ingenieurspsychologie*. Bern: Huber.
Hacker, W./Skell, W. (1993): *Lernen in der Arbeit*. Berlin: Bundesinstitut für Berufsbildung.
Harris, C./Daniels, K./Briner, R.B. (2003): A daily diary study of goals and affective well-being at work. In: *Journal of Occupational and Organizational Psychology*, 76, 3, pp. 401-410.
Harteis, C./Bauer, J./Gruber, H. (2008): The culture of learning from mistakes: How employees handle mistakes in everyday work. In: *International Journal of Educational Research*, 47, pp. 223-231.
Heckhausen, H./Beckmann, J. (1990): Intentional action and action slips. *In: Psychological Review*, 97, 1, pp. 36-48.
Ilgen, D.R./Fisher, C.D./Taylor, M.S. (1979): Consequences of individual feedback on behavior in organizations. In: *Journal of Applied Psychology*, 64, 4, pp. 349-371.
Laireiter, A.-R./Baumann, U./Reisenzein, E./Untner, A. (1997): A diary method for the assessment of interactive social networks: The interval-contingent diary SONET-T. In: *Swiss Journal of Psychology*, 56, 4, pp. 217-238.
Leventhal, H./Scherer, K. (1987): The relationship of emotion to cognition: A functional approach to a semantic controversy. In: *Cognition and Emotion*, 1, 1, pp. 3-28.
Loukidou, L./Loan-Clarke, J./Daniels, K. (2009): Boredom in the workplace: More than monotonous tasks. In: *International Journal of Management Reviews*, 11, 4, pp. 381-405.
Noss, M./Achtenhagen, F. (2002): Opportunities of supporting self-directed learning at the workplace – An empirical research on the training of bank employees. In: Beck, K. (ed.): *Teaching-Learning Processes in Vocational Education*. Frankfurt: Peter Lang, pp. 225-247.
Ohly, S./Sonnentag, S./Niessen, C./Zapf, D. (2010): Diary studies in organizational research. In: *Journal of Personnel Psychology*, 9, 2, pp. 79-93.
Oser, F. (2007): Aus Fehlern lernen. In: Göhlich, M./Wulf, C./Zirfas, J. (eds.): *Pädagogische Theorien des Lernens*. Weinheim: Beltz, pp. 203-212.
Prenzel, M. (1994): *Fragebogen zu motivationalen Bedingungen und zu motivationalen Prozessen beim Lernen*. Research Report (unpublished).
Rasmussen, J. (1982): Human errors. A taxonomy for describing human malfunction in industrial installations. In: *Journal of Occupational Accidents*, 4, pp. 311-333.

Rasmussen, J. (1983): Skills, rules, and knowledge; signals, signs, and symbols, and other distinctions in human performance models. In: *IEEE Transactions on Systems, Man, and Cybernetics*, 13, 3, pp. 257-266.
Rausch, A. (2011): *Erleben und Lernen am Arbeitsplatz in der betrieblichen Ausbildung*. Wiesbaden: VS-Verlag.
Reason, J.T. (1990): *Human error*. Cambridge: Cambridge University Press.
Rybowiak, V./Garst, H./Frese, M./Batinic, B. (1999): Error orientation questionnaire (EOQ): Reliability, validity, and different language equivalence. In: *Journal of Organizational Behavior*, 20, 4, pp. 527-547.
Scherer, K. (1994): Emotion serves to decouple stimulus and response. In: Ekman, P./Davidson, R. (eds.): *The Nature of Emotion*. New York: Oxford University Press, pp. 127-130.
Sembill, D. (1992): *Problemlösefähigkeit, Handlungskompetenz und Emotionale Befindlichkeit – Zielgrößen forschenden Lernens*. Göttingen: Hogrefe.
van Dyck, C./Frese, M./Baer, M./Sonnentag, S. (2005): Organizational error management culture and its impact on performance: A two-study replication. In: *Journal of Applied Psychology*, 90, 6, pp. 1228-1240.
Zapf, D./Reason, J.T. (1994): Introduction: Human errors and error handling. In: *Applied Psychology: An International Review*, 43, 4, pp. 427-432.
Zhao, B./Olivera, F. (2006): Error reporting in organizations. In: *Academy of Management Review*, 31, 4, pp. 1012-1030.

8 Professional Handling of Errors in the Workplace

Alexander Baumgartner and Jürgen Seifried

8.1 Introduction

The core element of the German vocational training system is the "dual system", which combines workplace learning with that in vocational schools. Workplace learning is of great importance for the development of apprentices' professional competence (Billett 2001; Fuller/Unwin 2003; Tynjäla 2008). In order to attain the benefits of an authentic working environment (i.e. fit of learning content and work requirements, minimal barriers of learning transfer), learning and working processes have to be integrated into implementation. This view attributes the quality of teaching-learning processes to the company trainers (Kirpal/Wittig 2009; Cedefop 2010). In spite of the relevance of trainers and the great range of learning and working in a training company in dual vocational training, this is not reflected in current research (Beck 2005). In contrast to research efforts in (vocational) school settings (q.v. Türling/Seifried/Wuttke in this edition), desiderata and gaps in knowledge can be identified. For example, little is known about staff training, which develops lower pedagogical competences than school teacher training. Moreover, the question of fostering the learning possibilities in the workplace has not been fully investigated, particularly with regard to learning from errors (Bauer 2008; Bauer/Mulder 2008; Gartmeier et al. 2008).

The article at hand elaborates both research desiderata in a discussion of how company trainers deal with apprentice errors within the German dual vocational training system. As work is usually to complex to totally eliminate the potential for errors (e.g. Senders/Moray 1991; van Dyck et al. 2005), dealing with errors in the workplace is an important strategy for workplace learning (Harteis/Bauer/Gruber 2008). Under the premise that it is generally possible to acquire vocational skills by learning from errors, the presumed learning potential can be realised, particularly if company trainers deal with error situations constructively (Oser/Spychiger 2005). Therefore, company trainers should be able to diagnose errors and their causes as well as handle the errors in order to foster learning. Despite enthusiasm for the workplace as a learning venue, we cannot overlook the fact that economic goals are paramount. Thus, from an economic point of view, error situations are the most important to be avoided. However, if errors occur, it should be possible to benefit from them (Yerushalmi/Polingher 2006).

8.2 Professional Competence of Company Trainers

8.2.1 Professional Pedagogical Competence of Company Trainers

In comparison with teachers at vocational schools, the characteristics and pedagogical competence of company trainers are not easy to describe. There are difficulties in determining their activities and positions in detail. Company trainers deal with a permanent state of tension between working reality and educational need. Conflicts of interests may arise as a result of divergent goals between entrepreneurs (VET in terms of costs) and trainees (VET in terms of learning and development). In addition, training efforts are not always considered in the assignment of activities; often leading to greater time pressure (Billett 2003:113).

Furthermore, there is a lack of clarity regarding (pedagogical) demands on trainers: when addressing teachers at vocational schools, on describing the additional tasks, people often speak about a "new" role, which implies a change in job profiles (Cedefop 2010). The key activity in training moves from a pure transfer of knowledge to the initiation and creation of learning processes; the trainer changes from an instructor to a tutor. This "new" role requires, apart from professional skills and abilities, a pedagogical competency, which is significantly more than what is required by the daily routine.

The quality of in-company training in the workplace depends not least on the professional qualifications of the training staff. Accordingly, firms entrust professionally qualified employees with training matters. However, this selection procedure is problematic because not every expert automatically has a sufficient degree of pedagogical knowledge and skill. Furthermore, studies on teacher competency from the school sector illustrate that pedagogical content knowledge (and not primarily the content knowledge themselves) is crucial for the success of pedagogical action (COACTIV study, Baumert et al. 2010). In contrast, occupational experience does not contribute to the clarification of teaching success. If these findings also apply to the in-company training sector, the question arises: where and when do trainers obtain pedagogical content knowledge? The question to be addressed here is whether and to what extent the regulations of 'Vocational Training Act' (Berufsbildungsgesetz), in combination with the 'Ordinance of Trainer Aptitude' (Ausbilder-Eignungsverordnung), are able to help with this process. Broadly speaking, two methods of competence acquisition exist: (1) pedagogical qualification through activity as trainer (*award*) and (2) pedagogical qualification through an institutionalised educational programme (*aptitude test*). Both possibilities are regarded as critical. Given the lack of pedagogic skills in the *pedagogical qualification through work experience,* a tendency to revert to a naive concept of good vocational training is feared. Individual experiences then become the point of reference for the creation of the teaching-learning processes.

In contrast, a *pedagogical qualification within the framework of an educational programme* aims for vocational education skills in addition to a professional qualification; but even this path cannot guarantee a comprehensive pedagogical qualification. For example, the 'Ordinance of Trainer Aptitude' provides no content differentiation between industry- and company-specific requirements. Moreover, the definition of company-trainer, i.e. who is entitled to carry out training measures by law and therefore needs vocational education skills, is not explicitly defined. It is common practice to only consider those registered as responsible trainers by the chamber as actual trainers. Skilled workers responsible for providing training on the job, however, are seldom pedagogically trained. As a result, trainers who are directly responsible for training in the workplace do not need a pedagogical certificate and an acknowledged full-time trainer provides no training, at least not at the learning venue workplace.

Assuming that company training staff do not have consistent formal pedagogical qualifications, the question arises, of what standards their pedagogical actions are based on. As such, personal experiences or proven common knowledge should lead the way because any didactic action – whether implicit or explicit – is based on beliefs of teaching and learning. In this connection, the terms personal epistemology (e.g. Hofer/Pintrich 1997; Stahl/Bromme 2007), conceptions of teaching and learning (e.g. Kember 1997) or subjective theories (e.g. Groeben/ Scheele 2001) have to be taken into account. Research on workplace learning has received (rather sporadic) attention in this area for more or less 30 years. Accordingly, a number of studies exist which provide an insight into vocational education and training. Of particular note is a Swiss study on company trainers' conceptions of teaching and learning in the commercial sector. The authors identify a link between conceptions of teaching and learning, trainers' actions and the quality of vocational training situations (Baeriswyl/Wandeler/Oswald 2006). Further studies show that only a few trainers direct their pedagogical action outside of their individual sphere of experience and that vocational training arrangements are based on operational and professional requirements (temporal and organisational conditions, degree of workload, personality characteristics of trainees) rather than pedagogical aspects (e.g. Brooker/Butler 1997; Harris/Simons/Bone 2006; for a systematisation of several approaches on the relevance of views of teaching and learning see Seifried/Baumgartner in press). All in all, empirical findings underline the assumption that individual beliefs of teaching and learning determine the actions of trainers in in-company training.

8.2.2 Trainer's Competences which Foster Error Learning

In the following we focus on a specific facet of company trainers' competence: supporting learning from errors in work situations. Reflections on whether and how one can learn from errors and how teaching staff deal with learners' errors are finding growing consideration in teaching-learning-research. The idea that errors can have a potential for learning was rarely supported at first (e.g. Weimer 1925). However, in recent years many doubts have been raised as to whether the negative assessment and sanction of errors in pedagogical contexts is the most effective approach (Yerushalmi/Polingher 2006). Of course it is necessary to differentiate between learning situations and work situations. While it is easy to agree that errors in learning processes might help knowledge acquisition, errors in working life, especially in high-risk-domains such as piloting an airplane or the operation of chemical and nuclear plants, have to be avoided. Due to the far-reaching consequences of human errors in these fields, it is not surprising that research projects in particular can be found in the accident- and safety industry. However, in reality errors with moderate consequences are more frequent and work is usually to complex to avoid them totally (Utler 2006) (at least not in in-company training). According to one of the few existing studies in the German dual vocational education and training system by Kutscha/Besener/Debie (2009) almost every apprentice in retail (n = 506) reports that errors in the workplace do occur and that these are often perceived as emotionally stressful. Thus, competence in dealing with errors during on-the-job training seems to be fundamental for the success of workplace learning in initial vocational education and training. Moreover, some empirical evidence shows a positive relationship between organisational error management culture and firm performance (van Dyck et al. 2005). So, constructive error management in companies requires responsive strategies (Nordstrom/Wendland/Williams 1998).

In teaching-learning research, the effect of feedback following errors is drawing increasing consideration. In school settings, there is evidence proving that the teachers' reaction to student errors is crucial to the learning process (to avoid making students feel foolish, to provide a positive atmosphere for errors and to give constructive response to errors). This also applies to on-the-job training: The attributed learning potential in error situations is particularly able to unfold, if the social relations in the working environment of trainees are perceived in a positive light (emotional component) and learning and reflection activities are stimulated (cognitive component) (Edmondson 1999; Ellström 2001; Rybowiak et al. 1999). Learning from errors, thus, is closely linked to company trainers' competence in handling apprentices' errors constructively. Therefore, we analyse the following three facets of trainers' error competence that are central to our research (q.v. Baumgartner/Seifried 2011):

1. *Understanding and knowledge of common apprentice errors difficulties in learning:* First, trainers have to actually recognise the specific logical flaws and false assumptions made by apprentices. To do this, trainers need domain-specific knowledge about possible learner errors.
2. *Understanding and knowledge of strategies for dealing with those errors and difficulties:* After having recognised the error, trainers must treat it "adequately". For this they have to know about alternatives of action (e.g. about giving feedback or when it is better to ignore errors).
3. *Belief regarding the benefit of dealing with apprentices' errors:* Roughly speaking, a so-called error-prevention-didactic (errors are to be prevented so that false trains of thought do not become habitual) can be set against a constructive management of errors. In this sense, trainers are prepared to become involved in students errors even if there are time constraints.

The learning potential in error situations can actually develop and result in knowledge acquisition if deeper reasons for errors are analysed and reflected on and if constructive feedback is given on how to improve in the future. Company trainers should be able to support such processes; but both the extent to which this is possible, and whether the necessary time and space is granted alongside their priority tasks depends, above all, on the trainers' opinion of errors (flaw versus learning opportunity).

8.3 Concept of an Empirical Study for Measuring Company Trainers' Error Competence

8.3.1 Short Description of the Chosen Domain

Errors always have to be regarded in the context of specific contents and demands, thus, the research question presented here requires a domain-specific approach. For the analysis of trainers' error competence an empirical study is being conducted in the domain of gastronomy and hotel business. Here, we focus on the in- company training within the German dual system of vocational education and training. The first reason for selecting this domain is that handling of errors is an urgent issue in hotel business to ensure the employment of sufficient numbers of qualified staff (high drop-out rate, low demand for training places and high proportion of young people with learning disabilities). Conversations with representatives from the hotel business confirm the great relevance of the topic. Secondly, the highly standardised nature of the work processes facilitates the identification of errors and is thus well suited to the discussion of errors:

- *Transparency in work processes:* Usually, there are concrete guidelines and schemes of how to do a task (e.g. cleaning of rooms, table setting, etc.). Hence, errors are recognisable and may be identified as such. Moreover, the criteria for judging actions as errors are mostly transparent.
- *Moderate consequences:* Errors do occur (and can hardly be avoided in fast-paced daily business or in rush hours) but do not entail serious (life-threatening) consequences.
- *Fast feedback:* The guests expect a trouble-free service process. It may be assumed that after an error in close contact with visitors the apprentice gets a prompt feedback of the guest himself or from superiors.

The noted considerations (transparency in the work processes, moderate consequences and fast feedback) seem to be important conditions for learning from errors. So, usable results are to be expected in the selected branch.

8.3.2 Research Questions

The study aims to analyse the professional action of company trainers for a specific facet of competence (dealing with apprentices' errors constructively). The project basically consists of the following two questions:

(1) Specification of possible domain-specific apprentice errors in the hotel business: As the first step, domain-specific errors were identified in a preliminary study. Relevant preliminary work was not already available in this field. For this we chose an empirical approach (expert interviews with n = 11 trainers with several years of experience in in-company training and 12 apprentices). The information about error types generated by the survey formed the starting point for the development of our central measuring instrument in the main study (representation of "typical" error situations in the form of photo sequences, so called picture vignettes, see chapter 3.3) (cf. Seifried/Baumgartner 2009).

(2) Modelling of company trainers' error competence: When modelling the company trainers' professional error competence we will focus on three components: (1) knowledge of possible error types in work situations, (2) available strategies of action/ trainers' reactions in error situations and their (3) personal views of the benefit/damage of errors.

The competence level is to examine whether there are correlations between the various components of the error competence. Furthermore, differences concerning error competence, depending on the level of (pedagogical) qualification and varying integration in the training processes or the work area have to be clarified. Respectively, we use a multistage research design, or rather, the combination of different research methods (mixed methods, cf.

Tashakkori/Teddlie 2003, see Seifried/Baumgartner in press).

8.3.3 Error-prone Activities and the Development of a Measuring Instrument

The preliminary study presented in this chapter contributes to the development of the central measurement instrument for handling of errors in the main study (picture vignettes). Since the case that errors have to be regarded in concrete situations has already been made, above, the goal is to identify specific apprentice errors for the domain hotel business. These errors are essential to the development of authentic situations that can be used as stimulus material for the implementation of the vignette-based approach.

For identifying "typical" apprentice errors, expert interviews were conducted by the authors. A semistructured interview guideline (in-depth interviews) was used, in which both the wording and the sequence of the question was variable and could be adjusted during conversation. The interview questions refer to the experience of the respondents in error situations (Examples: "Which work areas are particularly error-prone?", "Which errors occur frequently?"). Information from conversations with 11 company trainers and 12 apprentices is available. We used both groups as experts, because it can be assumed that not only trainers, but also learners, provide knowledge about common problematic situations in the work process of trainees.

The interviews were recorded, transcribed verbatim and analysed. The analysis is based on the principles of qualitative content analysis by Mayring (2003). The data were evaluated by two independent raters with the help of the text analysis software MAXQDA. The inter-rater reliability for 10 randomly chosen interviews (five interviews from trainers and five from apprentices) was substantial to almost perfect ($.68 \leq$ Cohen's Kappa $\leq .86$). Figure 1 shows the results of the expert interviews. For the error situations, a deductive categorisation strategy was followed. The statements on error-prone activities were allocated, on the one hand, to the different areas of work (service, kitchen, reception) and, on the other hand, to categories of activity (in total 17 categories based on the curriculum [description of activities] of the initial vocational hotel training plan). The number of mentions (value in front of the brackets) and the number of respondents, who named the respective aspect (value in the brackets), are listed. In total, 472 codings flow into the analysis. The represented categories in the illustration include over 90 % of the statements.

With regard to common errors, dealing with guests (work area *service*) is the most frequently reported category. This is true for the training staff as well as for the apprentices (in total 83 mentions of 18 respondents). In particular, poor communication or visitor care, insufficient processing of complaints as well as inappropriate behaviour towards guests are often described as "typical" errors. Also, tasks like waiting and table setting are seen as error-prone activities. In the work area *kitchen,* most errors occur during food preparation (56 mentions of 10 respondents). Moreover, experts point out that hygiene regulations are disregarded (also in *service*) and duty of care when receiving goods is neglected. In analogy to *service*, aspects of poor guest care and communication rank first in the work area *reception* (53 men-

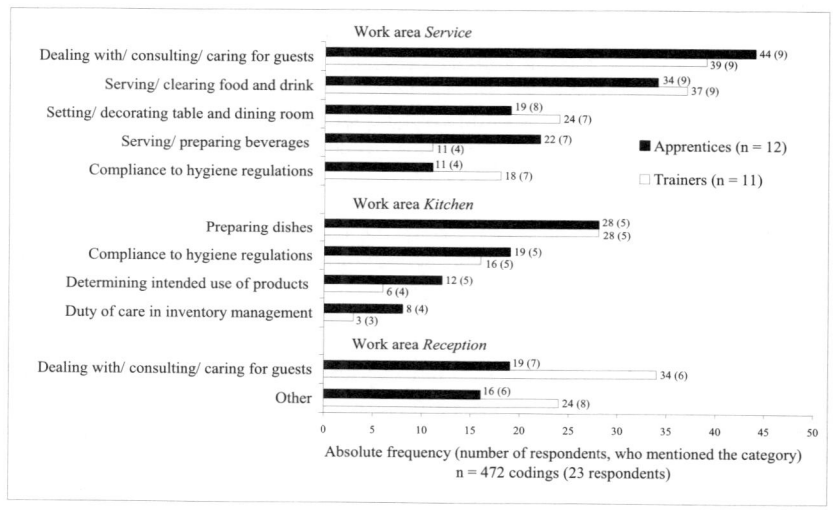

tions of 13 respondents).

Figure 1: Error-prone work areas in the hotel business

Source: own diagram

The statements of trainees and trainers about error-prone activities illustrate many similarities. This effect, although unexpected, points out that both "parties" obviously have a similar understanding of error-prone activities in work processes. Bearing in mind the objective of the expert interviews (identify and collect domain-specific apprentice errors for developing a measuring instrument for the main study), this empirical findings simplified the decision for the selection of error situations to be used in the pictorial representations.

On the basis of the results of the expert interviews we produced two vignettes for each work area. In order to analyse trainers' action in error situations under controlled conditions, stimuli are needed. This can be achieved through picture vignettes (photo sequences with four to eight pictures which contain text based information of the context in the represented scene), in which "typical" error-prone actions from trainees are imitated by actors. In general, vignettes can be described as short stories which can be represented in written, verbal, video-based or, as in our study, pictorial form. It is an instrument for detecting information about the attitudes and perceptions of respondents. For the development of vignettes, care should be taken to ensure that they are plausible and realistic, and contain enough content-specific information. In addition, the scenarios should reflect subjectively relevant everyday events and illustrate personal experiences of the respondents (Lanza/Carifio 1992; Barter/Renold 1999; Veal 2002). As an example, figure 2 shows two pictures from different vignettes (service/kitchen). Following critical actions can be found here: In the first picture the apprentice touches the wine glass at the bowl instead of the stern, the hygiene regulations are hence ignored (picture 2.1). In the second picture the hand posture is wrong when cutting meat, with this work technique the trainee's fingertips are in danger (picture 2.2).

By using picture vignettes, all of the respondents' statements based on comparable error situations. However, the definition of what is seen as an error in a specific context may differ among participants although the work processes in the described domain are highly standardised (cf. chapter 3.1). For this reason, we use the term "critical action" in the survey. So, an issue will not be seen exclusively in the context of generally accepted standards, but also within company-specific agreements. Therefore, the respondents involved in the survey judge for themselves, which "critical action" they categorise as an error or a deviation from the standard.

Figure 2: Example pictures of two vignettes

Source: own diagram

8.3.4 First Findings: How Trainers Diagnose Errors and Respond to them

In the course of competence measurement, we present picture vignettes to trainers and apprentices. The respondents look at two picture vignettes each out of their work area (trainer) or from the field of activity, in which they have mainly worked (apprentice). The respondents will be asked (in-depth interview) about available modes of behaviour or reactions in error situations (Examples: "How would you react in this work situation?", "Why did you choose this strategy?"). In addition, we want to analyse which of the embedded critical actions are identified, or rather categorised, as errors and what trainers know about the various causes of apprentice errors. In an initial data assessment we focus on particular parts of the first and second facet of trainers' error competence (cf. chapter 3.2): the ability to diagnose critical actions, or rather, error situations (1.) as a precondition for feedback (2.). To support trainees in error situations, trainers should be able to give elaborate feedback (Seifried/Wuttke 2010). A high level of elaboration during feedback is identified if, in addition to a statement of right or wrong, example explanations that help learners to understand both *why* an action was wrong and *how* it could be improved are given.

So far, we have carried out interviews with 72 respondents (38 trainers and 36 apprentices) in 16 hotels. In the following, we report the first impressions of work in progress based on 18 interviews with trainers (respondent 1 to 6: work area service [S]; respondent 7 to 14: work area kitchen [K], respondent 15 to 18: work area reception [R]):

(1) The trainers questioned (n = 18) could have found a total of 104 critical actions (18 respondents x 2 vignettes x 2 to 4 critical actions per vignette); in total 92 were identified. All critical situations were mentioned at least once. This indicates a distinct ability to diagnose errors in work situations. Six respondents detected all critical situations; whereas, 15 out of 18 company trainers identified more than half of the critical situations. Due to many years of experience in work and in-company training, this finding is not surprising. The work situations characterised as critical actions by us were regarded as deviation of the norm by a majority of respondents (81 out of 104). This finding might be due to the fact that most of the actions are based on transparent rules. In the other cases the actions were partly perceived as debatable but not as errors in the sense on which trainers necessarily have to react.

(2) With regard to available strategies of action in error situations, we examined the extent of feedback elaboration in more detail (cf. table 1). In total, trainers would give feedback for 74 of the 81 actions categorised as error (ignoring five). In two error cases a trainer did not want to report his

reaction. In a primary analysis (more detailed analyses are in progress) using dichotomous coding (yes/no), we analysed whether the trainers' feedback includes, firstly, information about *error analysis* and, secondly, hints for *error correction*. In about one third of all cases (24 out of 74) both conditions are fulfilled. In the current state of analysis trainers' reactions indicate only little variance. 15 of 18 respondents demonstrate a high level of elaboration in at least one error situation (five respondents in two and two respondents in three). In the remaining feedback there is, in particular in the kitchen, often a lack of error analysis. The respondents communicated, however, more frequently information about error correction, (by all respondents in 58 of 74 cases). A distinction of trainers' behaviour can be made between the work areas. It seems that errors in work areas with a lot of personal contact with guests (reception, service) are analysed more precisely. One reason for this may be the fact that it is hard for apprentices to assess guests' different needs and, therefore, errors have to be clarified in the specific context. Moreover, the level of difficulty of the action appears to have an influence on trainers' reactions. It can be assumed that errors in relatively simple "routine activities" are more rarely analysed because one can expect apprentices to already know the causes of their own misconduct. Further analyses have to be made in order to adequately answer the question about feedback quality. Moreover, apprentices' statements have to be integrated so that the critical actions of all participants in the training process are taken into account.

Table 1: Feedback in error situations

Respond.	Error situation		Extent of elaboration during feedback				Condition (1) & (2) in x of (y) cases fulfilled
			Condition (1) Error analysis		Condition (2) Error correction		
	fed back	ignored	yes	No	yes	No	
P 1	3	-	-	3	2	1	- (3)
P 2	4	-	3	1	3	1	2 (4)
P 3	5	-	2	3	5	-	2 (5)
P 4	2	1	1	1	0	2	0 (2)
P 5	6	-	4	2	5	1	3 (6)
P 6	6	-	3	3	4	2	3 (6)
Sum (S)	26	1	13	13	19	7	10 (26)
P 7	4	1	1	3	3	1	1 (4)
P 8	3	1	2	1	3	-	2 (3)
P 9	4	1	1	3	4	-	1 (4)
P 10	4	-	2	2	4	-	2 (4)
P 11	4	-	1	3	4	-	1 (4)
P 12	4	-	1	3	3	1	1 (4)
P 13	5	-	1	4	5	-	1 (5)
P 14	4	-	1	3	3	1	0 (4)
Sum (K)	32	3	10	22	29	3	9 (32)

Table 1: Feedback in error situations (cont.)

Respond.	Error situation		Extent of elaboration during feedback				Condition (1) & (2) in x of (y) cases fulfilled
			Condition (1) *Error analysis*		Condition (2) *Error correction*		
	fed back	ignored	yes	No	yes	No	
P 15	3	-	3	-	1	2	1 (3)
P 16	4	1	3	1	4	-	2 (4)
P 17	4	-	4	-	1	3	1 (4)
P 18	5	-	2	3	4	1	1 (5)
Sum (R)	16	1	12	4	10	6	5 (16)
Total	74	5	35	39	58	16	24 (74)

Note. (S) = Service, (K) = Kitchen, (R) = Reception

Source: own table

8.4 Summary and Outlook

After an erroneous action apprentices should obtain constructive feedback. This is especially necessary, if apprentices do not (immediately) realise the consequences of their own action in complex and/or new work situations. Well-founded knowledge of common apprentice errors in work processes are preconditions for constructive feedback. First findings show a rather high level of competence in apprentices' error recognition. To what extent these findings depend on professional experience in work and in-company training has yet to be analysed. In order to be able to evaluate the strategies of dealing with errors with respect to effectiveness, it is essential to describe and classify the error situations in the picture vignettes in detail. We assume that the complexity and difficulty as well as the consequences and reversibility of an (erroneous) action influence trainers' reaction in error situations. Moreover, feedback quality has to be considered in greater detail. An important aspect is the timing of feedback. In the literature, a prompt feedback is considered most beneficial (Kulik/Kulik 1988) so that false trains of thought are quickly corrected and uncertainties are prevented. Beyond that, the question arises whether the feedback refers to the incorrect action or to the apprentice (Kluger/DeNisi 1996).

In the further course of the project, we will extend the theoretical framework, the data evaluation and complete the sample. The integration of the apprentices' statements into the analysis will ensure that the picture vignettes are taken into account from the perspective of each of the training process participant groups. In addition, we will employ an adaption of the Error Orientation Questionnaire (Rybowiak et al. 1999) to analyse trainers' beliefs about learning from errors. Finally, it is highly advantageous that we are currently pursuing a thematically similar project with teachers in vocational schools (q.v. Türling/Seifried/Wuttke in this edition); thereby, enabling a direct comparison between schools' teaching staff and company trainers.

References

Baeriswyl, F./Wandeler, C./Oswald, K. (2006): *Die Ausbildungskonzeptionen von betrieblichen Ausbildenden – Schlussbericht des Teilprojektes Freiburg. Qualitätsmerkmale und ihre Wirkung in der betrieblichen Bildung (QuWibB)*. Research Report (unpublished).
Barter, C./Renold, E. (1999): The use of vignettes in qualitative research. In: *Social Research Update 25*. Surrey: University of Surrey/Department of Sociology. Retrieved April 11, 2011, from http://sru.soc.surrey.ac.uk/SRU25.html.
Baumert, J./Kunter, M./Blum, W./Brunner, M./Voss, T./ Jordan, A./Klusmann, U./ Krauss, S./Neubrand, M./ Tsai, Y.-M. (2010): Teachers' mathematical knowledge, cognitive activation in the classroom, and student progress. In: *American Educational Research Journal*, 47, 1, pp. 133-180.
Baumgartner, A./Seifried, J. (2011): Umgang mit Fehlern am Arbeitsplatz: Das Beispiel Gastronomie. In: *BWP – Berufsbildung in Wissenschaft und Praxis*, 40, 1, pp. 20-24.
Bauer, J./Mulder, R.H. (2008): Conceptualising learning from errors at work: A literature review. In: Billett, S./Harteis, C./Eteläpelto, A. (eds.): *Emerging perspectives on learning through work*. Rotterdam: Sense, pp. 115-128.
Bauer, J. (2008): *Learning from errors at work. Studies on nurses' engagement in error-related learning activities*. Ph.D. thesis. Regensburg: University of Regensburg/Institute of Education.
Beck, K. (2005): Ergebnisse und Desiderate zur Lehr-Lern-Forschung der der kaufmännischen Berufsausbildung. In: *Zeitschrift für Berufs- und Wirtschaftspädagogik*, 101, 4, pp. 533-556.
Billett, S. (2003): Workplace mentors: demands and benefits. In: *Journal of Workplace Learning*, 15, 3, pp. 105-113.
Billett, S. (2001): *Learning in the workplace: strategies for effective practice*. Sydney: Allen & Unwin.
Brooker, R./Butler, J. (1997): The learning context within the workplace: as perceived by apprentices and their workplace trainers. In: *Journal of Vocational Education & Training*, 49, 4, pp. 487-510.
Cedefop (2010): *Professional development opportunities for in-company trainers. A compilation of good practices*. Luxembourg: Publications Office of the European Union. Retrieved April 11, 2011, from http://www.cedefop.europa.eu/EN/Files/6106_en.pdf.
Edmondson, A.C. (1999): Psychological safety and learning behaviour in work teams. In: *Administrative Science Quarterly*, 44, 2, pp. 350-383.

Ellström, P.-E. (2001): Integrating learning and work: Problems and prospects. In: *Human Resource Development Quarterly*, 12, 4, pp. 421-435.
Eraut, M. (1994): *Developing professional knowledge and competence.* London: Routledge Falmer.
Fuller, A./Unwin, L. (2003): Fostering workplace learning: Looking through the lens of apprenticeship. In: *European Educational Research Journal*, 2 (1), pp. 41-55.
Gartmeier, M./Bauer, J./Gruber, H./Heid, H. (2008): Negative knowledge: Understanding professional learning and expertise. In: *Vocations and Learning*, 1, 2, pp. 87-103.
Groeben, N./Scheele, B. (2001): Dialogue-hermeneutic method and the "Research Program Subjective Theories". In: *Forum Qualitative Sozialforschung/Forum: Qualitative Social Research*, 1, 2. Retrieved April 11, 2011, from http://www.qualitative-research.net/ index. php/ fqs/article/viewArticle/1079/2353.
Harris, R./Simons, M./Bone, J. (2006): *Mix or match? New apprentices' learning styles and trainers' preferences for training in workplaces.* Adelaide: NCVER.
Harteis, C./Bauer, J./Gruber, H. (2008): The culture of learning from mistakes: how employees handle mistakes in everyday work. In: *International Journal of Educational Research*, 47, 4, pp. 223–231.
Hofer, B.K./ Pintrich, P.R. (1997): The development of epistemological theories. Beliefs about knowledge and knowing and their relation to learning. In: *Review of Educational Research*, 67, 1, pp. 88-140.
Kember, D. (1997): A reconceptualisation of the research into university academics' conceptions of teaching. In: *Learning and Instruction*, 7, 3, pp. 255-275.
Kirpal, S./Wittig, W. (2009): Training practitioners in Europe: Perspectives of their work, qualification and continuing learning. In: *ITB-Forschungsberichte 41.* Bremen: University of Bremen. Retrieved April 11, 2011, from http://elib.suub.uni-bremen.de/ip/docs/00010 607.pdf.
Kluger, A.N./DeNisi, A.S. (1996): The effects of feedback interventions on performance: A historical review, a meta-analysis, and a preliminary feedback intervention theory. In: *Psychological Bulletin*, 119, 2, pp. 254-284.
Kulik, J.A./Kulik, C.-L.C. (1988): Timing of feedback and verbal learning. In: *Review of Educational Research Journal*, 58, 1, pp. 79-97.
Kutscha, G./Besener, A./Debie, S.O. (2009): *Probleme der Auszubildenden in der Eingangsphase der Berufsausbildung im Einzelhandel – ProBE. Abschlussbericht und Materialien zum Forschungsprojekt.* Essen: University of Duisburg-Essen. Retrieved April 11, 2011, from http://www.uni-due.de/~hd257ku/probe/media/bericht/Projektbericht.pdf.
Lanza, M.L./Carifio, J. (1992): Use of a panel of experts to establish validity for patient assault vignettes. In: *Evaluation Review*, 16, 1, pp. 82-92.
Mayring, P. (2003): *Qualitative Inhaltsanalyse. Grundlagen und Techniken.* Weinheim: Beltz.
Nordstrom, C.R./Wendland, D./Williams, K.B. (1998): «To err is human»: an examination of the effectiveness of error management training. In: *Journal of Business and Psychology*, 12, 3, pp. 269–282.
Oser, F./Spychiger, M. (2005): *Lernen ist schmerzhaft. Zur Theorie des negativen Wissens und zur Praxis der Fehlerkultur.* Weinheim: Beltz.

Rybowiak, V./Garst, H./ Frese, M./Batinic, B. (1999): Error Orientation Questionnaire (EOQ): Reliability, validity and different language equivalence. In: *Journal of Organizational Behavior*, 20, 4, pp. 527–547.

Seifried, J./Baumgartner, A. (2009): Lernen aus Fehlern in der betrieblichen Ausbildung – Problemfeld und möglicher Forschungszugang. In: *Berufs- und Wirtschaftspädagogik – online*, 17. Retrieved April 11, 2011, from http://www.bwpat.de/ content/ uploads/media/seifried_baumgartner_bwpat17.pdf.

Seifried, J./Wuttke, E. (2010): Students' errors: how teachers diagnose them and how they respond to them. In: *Empirical Research in Vocational Education and Training (ERVET)*, 2, 2, pp. 147-162.

Seifried, J./Baumgartner, A. (in press): Professionelles Handeln von Ausbildungspersonen in Fehlersituationen. In: Weiß, R./Zöller, A./Ulmer, P. (eds.): *Herausforderungen an das Bildungspersonal in der beruflichen Aus- und Weiterbildung: Forschungsbefunde und Qualifizierungskonzepte*. Bielefeld: Bertelsmann.

Senders, J.W./Morray, N.P. (1991): *Human error – cause, prediction and reduction*. Hillsdale: L. Erlbaum Associates.

Stahl, E./Bromme, R. (2007): The CAEB: An instrument for measuring connotative aspects of epistemological beliefs. In: *Learning and Instruction*, 17, 6, pp. 773-785.

Tashakkori, A./Teddlie, C.B. (2003): *Handbook of mixed methods in social and behavioural research*. Thousands Oaks: Sage Publications.

Tynjälä, P. (2008): Perspectives into learning at the workplace. In: *Educational Research Review*, 3, 2, pp. 130-154.

Utler, C. (2006): Von der Schuldzuweisung zum Risikomanagement. In: Debatin, J.F./Goyen, M./Schmitz, C. (eds.): *Zukunft Krankenhaus – Überleben durch Innovation*. Berlin: ABW Wissenschaftsverlag, pp. 1-30.

van Dyck, C./Frese, M./Baer, M./Sonnentag, S. (2005): Organizational error management culture and its impact on performance: A two-study replication. In: *Journal of Applied Psychology*, 90, 6, pp. 1228–1240.

Weimer, H.(1925): *Psychologie der Fehler*. Leipzig: Klinkhardt.

Veal, W.R. (2002): Content specific vignettes as tools for research and training. In: *Electronic Journal of Science Education*, 6, 4, pp. 1-37.

Yerushalmi, E./Polingher, C. (2006): Guiding students to learn from mistakes. In: *Physics Education*, 41, 6, pp. 532-538.

9 Learning From Errors – Perspectives from Basic Research

Andy J. Wills

9.1 Introduction

Most of the chapters in this volume report ongoing applied research into learning from errors. This chapter is slightly different, in that it takes a step back and reflects on what some of the recent findings in basic research might contribute to the formulation and interpretation of future applied research. In this context, "basic research" denotes research whose primary purpose is to attempt to reveal basic underlying processes of learning, rather than to examine learning in a specific applied context.

Two themes in this volume are (1) the importance of errors in driving learning, and (2) the importance of elaborated feedback. In both cases, basic research both partly supports, and partly modifies, these themes. Many chapters also convey the reality that (3) learning new skills to a high level typically involves an extended period of error-prone practice. Again, basic research partly supports, and partly modifies, this view. In reviewing some basic research in these three areas, I hope to provide a source of potential hypotheses and interventions for future applied research into learning from errors.

9.2 The Importance of Errors

From an early 20th century view that errors are avoidable aberrations (Weimer 1925), applied research now seems to broadly consider errors as "important and precious steps within human development" (Link, this volume: 49), whilst of course acknowledging the costs of workplace errors (Zhao/Olivera 2006). Basic research provides strong support for the notion that errors drive learning, but the view of what constitutes an error seems to differ in basic and applied research.

One illustration of the essential relationship between learning and errors comes from the field of contingency learning. For the purposes of illustration, a single example is discussed here but the field itself is extensive; for relatively accessible reviews, see Wills (2005, 2009). In this example, imagine you are an allergist, trying to discover which of several foods (peas, carrots, chicken, ham) produce an allergic reaction in your patient. Figure 1 illustrates what you learn as a result of your investigation. Given the information in this figure, which do you think is more likely to cause an allergic reaction in the patient – chicken or ham?

Table 1: An illustrative cue-competition experiment

(1) First you learn ...	(2) Then you learn ...	(3) Then you're asked ...
Peas → Rash	Peas + chicken → Rash	Chicken → Rash?
Carrots → No rash	Carrots + ham → Rash	Ham → Rash?

Source: Wills 2009, 96

The most common response to this question is "ham". This is intriguing because, in both cases, you have seen the patient eat the food in question and develop a rash. You have seen this happen an equal number of times for each of the two foods. So, what underlies the belief that ham is more likely to cause an allergic reaction? It cannot be attributed to differences in prior beliefs about chicken and ham, because the result is also found with entirely artificial stimuli; for example the same result is found using meaningless abstract shapes as stimuli instead of foods (Wills/Lavric/Croft/Hodgson 2007).

The phenomenon at work, known as cue competition, is widely observed in humans and other animals (Shanks 1995), and is predicted by the hypothesis that we learn more from prediction errors than we do from prediction successes (see Pearce 2008, for a review; for a different perspective, see Mitchell/De Houwer/Lovibond 2009). A prediction error occurs when an event in the environment differs from our expectation. The concept of a prediction error roughly equates to the everyday concept of being surprised. We were not surprised that the patient developed a rash after eating peas and chicken, because we could already predict the presence of an allergic reaction on the grounds that he had eaten peas, which we already knew caused a rash. We therefore learned relatively little about the relationship between chicken and allergic reaction. In contrast, we were somewhat more surprised that the patient developed a rash after eating ham, and hence we learned more about the relationship between ham and allergic reaction.

In summary, research on the basic processes of learning supports the contention that errors drive learning. However, the definition of an error in this basic research seems different to the way errors are operationalized in applied research. Typically, an error in an applied setting is an action emitted by the learner which the teacher (or researcher) considers to be inappropriate. In other words, the notion of error in applied research seems to correspond to "doing wrong". In research on the basic principles of learning, the necessary component for driving learning is a prediction error, which corresponds to the everyday concept of "being surprised".

Clearly, it is possible to be surprised without doing wrong, and to do wrong without being surprised. Formal theories of learning generally consider that it is surprise, rather than the emission of inappropriate actions, that drives learning. In fact, there is some evidence that the optimal conditions for learning, at least in the laboratory, are those where surprise is retained but the potential for emitting inappropriate actions is minimized. Baddeley and Wilson (1994) compared two forms of training on a stem completion task. Stem completion involves completing a word from its initial letters. For example the stem "QU_ _ _" can be completed in a variety of ways; for example QUEST, QUEEN, QUIET or QUICK. For the purposes of Baddeley and Wilson's study one particular completion was randomly denoted as correct (e.g. for "QU _ _ _", "QUEEN" is denoted as correct). Baddeley and Wilson then compared errorful versus errorless training on a series of stem completions.

In errorful training, participants received instructions such as "I am thinking of a five-letter word beginning with QU. Can you guess what it might be?" The participant makes some guesses and, due to the large number of possible completions, those guesses are normally wrong. The participant receives feedback on their guess, "No, good guess, but the word is QUOTE. Please write that down". Hence, in errorful training, the participant is both surprised (in the sense of expectations being violated) and wrong (in the sense of emitting inappropriate responses).

In errorless training, participants receive instructions such as "I am thinking of a five-letter word ... and the word is QUOTE, please write that down". Hence, errorless training still involves an element of surprise (albeit, arguably lesser and more temporary surprise) but, crucially, errorless training minimizes the possibility that the participant generates an inappropriate response.

In a subsequent test, Baddeley and Wilson found that participants who had received errorless training performed more accurately than participants who had received errorful training. This errorless learning advantage is typically explained by the assumption that not only the correct response, but also the incorrect responses, enter into memory. Subsequently, the memories of previous errors can lead to further errors if the participant fails to identify source of the memory (i.e. that it is a memory of an error). The fact that source memory develops late (Brainerd/Stein/Reyna 1998), declines in old age, and deteriorates in young adults if they are multi-tasking (Jennings/ Jacoby 1993) means that errorful training is particularly likely to result in further errors where learners are young, old, or in demanding workplace environments.

9.3 The Importance of Elaborated Feedback

One of the recurring themes in this volume is the importance of elaborated feedback. As Baumgartner and Seifried (this volume) put it, in addition to a statement of right or wrong, feedback should also include statements about why the action was wrong and how it could be improved (see also Rausch, this volume). Basic research on learning supports, but also contextualizes, this theoretical position. Specifically, the issue of whether elaborated feedback is more, or less, helpful than minimal feedback appears to depend on which of two competing learning systems in the brain control behaviour for a particular task.

Recent neuroimaging and behavioural work supports the idea that there are at least two anatomically and functionally distinct learning modes in the normal adult human brain. This idea has many overlapping expressions (see e.g. Erickson/Kruschke 1998; Smith/Grossman 2008), and some detractors (e.g. Newell/Dunn/Kalish 2011). For brevity, I have focussed here on one of the most prominent recent accounts – the COVIS theory (see Ashby/Paul/Maddox 2011, for an accessible review). COVIS is an acronym, standing for COmpetition between Verbal and Implicit Systems. The acronym neatly encapsulates the idea that we have two systems of learning, and that these systems are in competition with each other. One system is the verbal system, located in the prefrontal cortex and anterior cingulate. This system learns through the generation and testing of verbalizable hypotheses about the world. The other system is the implicit system, which learns through the modification of simple connections from stimulus representations on the cortical surface, to response representations in the striatum. To caricature slightly, the verbal system is a smart learning system unique to, or at least characteristic of, adult human thought. The implicit system is an older, dumber, learning system that we likely share to some extent with most vertebrates. What, then, is the utility of the implicit system in, for example, workplace learning?

Figure 1: (A) Example of a category structure that can be easily verbalized. (B) Rotated by 45 degrees, the same abstract structure becomes very difficult to verbalize

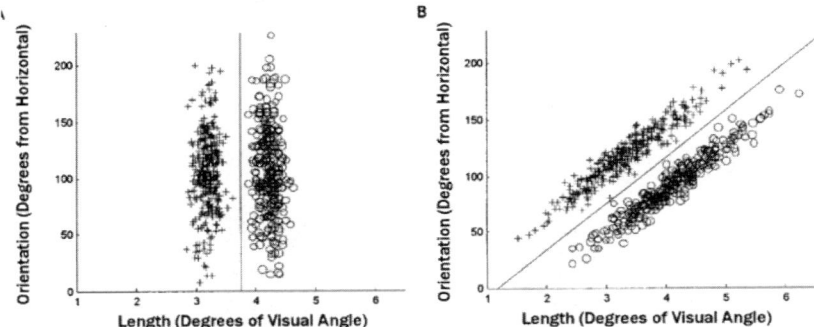

Source: Ashby/Ell/Waldron 2003, 1115

There are two answers to this question. First, the defining property of the verbal system is that the hypotheses it generates are constrained by what is verbalizable. Problems that are similar in an abstract sense can differ dramatically in the extent to which they are amenable to a compact verbal summary. For example, Figure 2 shows two category structures. Each of the two types of plot symbol (crosses, circles) represents one category of objects. The coordinates of each plot symbol represent one object shown to participants. The line represents the boundary between the two categories. The category structure shown in Figure 2A permits a concise verbal summary – category A objects are short, whilst category B objects are long. Of course, there is some fine learning involved in working out when "long" becomes "short" in this particular context. However, Figure 2B which, formally speaking, is just a rotation of the stimulus structure in Figure 2A, permits no simple verbal summary because the two dimensions are qualitatively different. In some abstract sense, category B objects are longer than they are slanted, but the absence of common units means such a description is not of much practical use (and would be unlikely to be discovered by the verbal system). So, the first answer to the question, "what is the implicit system good for?" is that it is good for learning things that are not easily verbalized. Whilst some skills and knowledge we attempt to impart in the classroom and workplace are easily verbalizable others, presumably, are not.

Another answer to the question, "what is the implicit system good for?" is that it is good for skills we wish to be executed quickly and/or to not be adversely affected by high pressure – for example, the requirement to multitask. The laboratory evidence indicates that tasks where the verbal system dominates are particularly error prone under a multi-tasking load, whilst tasks where the implicit system dominates are less affected by load (Waldron/ Ashby 2001).

Figure 2: Effects of extent of feedback on accuracy for two types of category structure

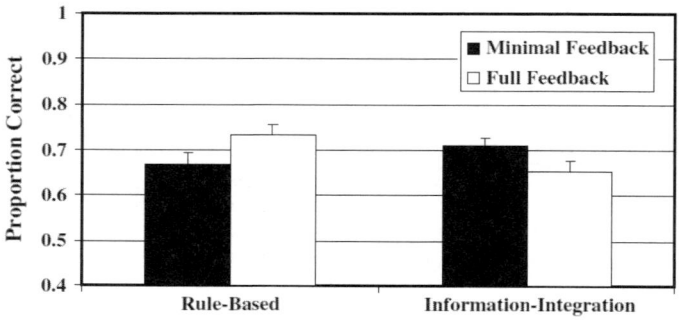

Source: Maddox/Love/Glass/Filoteo 2008, 585

Returning to the issue of the superiority of elaborated over minimal feedback, recent lab work suggests that tasks where the verbal system dominates are learned best with elaborated feedback, whilst tasks where the implicit system dominates are learned best with minimal feedback. Maddox, Love, Glass and Filoteo (2008), using category structures similar to those illustrated in Figure 2, compared the effects of elaborated versus minimal feedback on learning readily verbalized (Figure 2A) versus not readily verbalized (Figure 2B) category structures. In all conditions of the experiment, participants were presented with objects one at a time, and asked to say to which category they belonged. Each decision was followed by feedback, but this feedback was either minimal ("Correct" or "Wrong"), or somewhat more elaborated (e.g., "Correct, that belonged to Category A", "Wrong, that belonged to category B"). Of course, it is possible to think of forms of feedback that are more elaborate than this, but even this relatively moderate level of elaboration was sufficient to improve performance in a readily verbalizable problem (see Figure 3, "rule-based"). The striking result, however, was that full feedback led to worse performance than minimal feedback for non-verbalizable problems (Figures 3, "information-integration"). So, in some cases at least, less is more – less elaborated feedback leads to better performance. Why does this happen? Maddox et al. (2008) argue that the verbal system benefits from elaborated feedback, whilst the implicit system, which is a dumb reinforcement learning system, does not. Elaborated feedback can hurt performance in situations where it leads to the verbal system controlling behaviour for longer, despite the fact that – ultimately – the implicit system would produce more accurate responding (because it is not limited to structures that can be verbalized).

Expanding on this issue slightly, it is presumably sometimes the case in practice that generating and delivering elaborated feedback takes significantly longer than delivering minimal feedback. This isn't a problem where learning is dominated by the verbal system, because the verbal system is relatively impervious to delays between making a response and receiving feedback. However, even small delays in feedback can be a problem where the implicit system is controlling behaviour. For example, Maddox and Ing (2005) found that delaying feedback by 5 seconds in a non-verbalizable problem reduced accuracy by about 20 percentage points. A 5 second delay in feedback had no detectable effect on a readily verbalizable problem. Again, this pattern of results can be understood from the assumption that the implicit system is a dumb reinforcement learning mechanism. Such systems, due to their relatively simple construction, are strongly affected by the temporal contiguity of events.

In summary, basic research on feedback processes suggests that what is critical to ensure efficient learning is to match the feedback given to the properties of the mental system that is doing the learning. Where the learning takes the form of verbal hypothesis testing, elaborated feedback seems to be superior to minimal feedback. However, where the learning takes the form of dumb association, minimal feedback may be better, and immediacy of feedback is paramount. It is perhaps worth noting that many skills in which we are all expert (e.g. simple mental arithmetic) appear, once mastered, to substantially involve relatively dumb automatic retrieval processes (e.g. Logan 1988).

9.4 The Importance of Extended Practice

Learning anything worthwhile is hard, and it generally takes a long time. The necessity of extended practice is often illustrated by the 10,000 hours heuristic - over a wide variety of skills, one thing that unites those regarded as experts is that they have engaged in at least 10,000 hours of deliberate practice of that skill (e.g. Ericsson/Lehmann 1996). The 10,000 hour heuristic is thus a powerful empirical generalization, but the question remains – is extended practice, and the period of error-prone behaviour that accompanies it, an inevitable part of learning complex skills? Or can research on basic processes of learning indicate ways in which the efficiency of learning might substantially be increased?

One particularly striking example of success in this regard is Biederman and Shiffrar's (1987) study of the skill of day-old chick sexing. Intensive farming methods require a process by which chicks can be identified as male or female, very rapidly, and with very low error rates. The task is not trivial, and it takes several years of on-the-job practice to reach optimal levels of performance. Yet Biederman and Shiffrar were able to design a training session of just a few minutes duration that brought novices close to expert levels of performance. This impressive increase in training efficiency was achieved through what is described as an expert systems analysis of an individual with over 50 years of chicken sexing experience. Through this process, it was possible to produce highly caricatured versions of the critical discriminating features, as shown in Figure 4.

Figure 3: Top row: Magnified images of the genital eminences of day-old chicks; in real life, the critical features are approximately the size of a pin head. The two pictures on the left are male genitals, the two pictures on the right are female genitals; adapted from Canfield (1941). Bottom row: Carciatures of the critical features

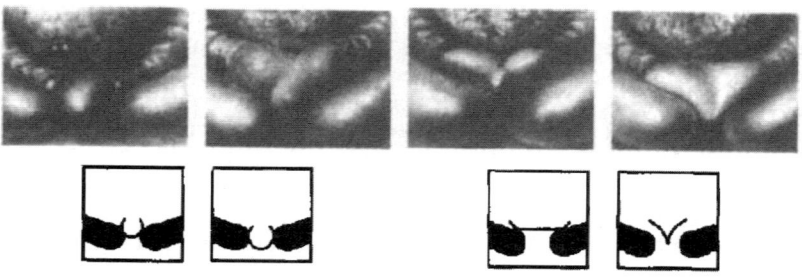

Source: Biedmann/Shiffrar 1987, 641

Nor is Biederman and Shiffrar's use of this caricaturing approach an isolated success. For example, native speakers of Japanese learning to speak English often find it difficult to discriminate between "l" and "r" sounds. This difficulty is understandable as, in Japanese, the sounds "l" and "r" are allophones (i.e. different sounds that denote the same phoneme). As an illustration of the difficulty of discriminating allophones, consider the words "pin" and "spin". Both contain a "p" sound but, in typical pronunciation, the "p" in "pin" is aspirated, whilst the "p" in spin is unaspirated. If you place your hand close to your mouth whilst saying these words, you should be able to detect a difference in air pressure. Most native English speakers are unaware of the difference between aspirated and unaspirated "p", because they are allophonic in English. In other languages they are allophones. For example, in Thai changing from an aspirated to an unaspirated "p" can change the meaning of a word. Caricaturing has been shown to be effective in accelerating the learning of the "l" versus "r" distinction. Using digital signal processing methods, it is possible to compare the frequency spectra of the "l" and the "r" sound, and then digitally enhance the differences between those sounds – effectively creating a super "l" and a super "r". Training programmes that start with these caricatured sounds and gradually move towards the real sounds lead to better performance than an equivalent amount of time spent training on the real sounds (McClelland/Fiez/McCandliss 2002).

One reason carciaturing might be so effective is that it provides a direct answer to one of the key problems faced by any system attempting to learn from errors – what, in the complex and rich problem space the learner faces, is the cause of their errors? To put it another way, caricaturing tells the learner what to look at (or listen to) – information that can be and is learned from prediction errors (Wills et al. 2007; Wills 2009) but which, at least where the distinctions are subtle to a novice, can be more effectively achieved through caricature. A caricature, in some sense, takes what is there in the world, and turns it into a representation of how a relevant expert sees it. It encapsulates one key part of learning from prediction errors into a readily communicable form. Note that one strength of caricatures is that their communicable form is potentially something from which both a verbal and an non-verbal learning system could benefit. Carciatures, in summary, may be one way of elaborating the learning experience that can benefit even hard-to-verbalize skills.

9.5 Conclusion

This chapter provides no ready-made solutions for increasing the efficiency of learning in specific applied contexts. Instead, it provides three evidence-based ideas that might serve as a source of hypotheses for applied research.

The first idea is that it is not errors, but surprise, that drives learning. Indeed, the commission of an error can lead to the perseveration of that error under certain circumstances. Training programmes that can retain surprise but minimize action errors may be particularly effective.

The second idea is that it is not how elaborated feedback is that determines its effectiveness, but how well it fits with the learning mode (verbal or non-verbal) that dominates in that particular task at a particular stage of learning. Verbal learning benefits from elaborate feedback, even if that feedback takes a little while to arrive. Non-verbal learning benefits from minimal feedback, and it is particularly important that the feedback arrives as close to the error as possible. In the lab, delays of even a few seconds can lead to substantial reductions in accuracy if the task depends on hard-to-verbalize knowledge.

The third idea is that for tasks novices find difficult and time-consuming to learn, it may be the case that a large part of the learning is not so much concerned with how to react when you come across a particular set of circumstances, but learning how to see the world in a different way such that you can identify the circumstances in the first place. People can and do learn how to see their expert domains through prediction-error-based learning, but caricatures can sometimes provide a powerful way to condense years of experience into a readily communicable form.

In the end, though, all three of these ideas are born mainly of theory and lab-based experimentation. I offer them in the hope that they may provide a useful starting point for projects of direct societal and/or economic impact.

References

Ashby, F.G./Ell, S.W./Waldron, E.M. (2003): Procedural learning in perceptual categorization. In: *Memory and Cognition,* 31, pp. 1114-1125.

Ashby, F.G./Paul, E. J./Maddox, W. T. (2011): COVIS. In: Pothos, E.M./Wills, A.J. (eds.): *Formal approaches in categorization.* Cambridge University Press.

Baddeley, A./Wilson, B.A. (1994): When implicit learning fails: Amnesia and the problem of error elimination. In: *Neuropsychologia,* 32, pp. 53-68.

Biederman, I./Shiffrar, M.M. (1987): Sexing day-old chicks: A case study and expert systems analysis of a difficult perceptual-learning task. In: *Journal of Experimental Psychology: Learning, Memory and Cognition,* 13, pp. 640-645.

Brainerd, C.J./Stein, L.M./Reyna, V.F. (1998): On the development of conscious and unconscious memory. In: *Developmental Psychology,* 34, pp. 342-357.

Canfield, T.H. (1940). Sex determination of day-old chicks. In: *Poultry Science,* 77, pp. 235-238.

Erickson, M.A./Kruschke, J.K. (1998): Rules and exemplars in category learning. In: *Journal Of Experimental Psychology: General,* 127, pp. 107-140.

Ericsson, K.A./Lehmann, A.C. (1996): Expert and exceptional performance: Evidence of maximal adaptation to task constraints. In: *Annual Review of Psychology,* 47, pp. 273-305.

Jennings, J.M./Jacoby, L.L. (1993): Automatic versus intentional uses of memory: Aging, attention and control. In: *Psychology and Aging,* 8, pp. 283-293.

Logan, G.D. (1988). Toward an instance theory of automatization. In: *Psychological Review,* 95, pp. 492-527.

Maddox, W.T./Love, B.C./Glass, B.D./Filoteo, J.V. (2008): When more is less: Feedback effects in perceptual category learning. In: *Cognition,* 108, pp. 578-589.

McClelland, J.L./Fiez, J.A./McCandliss, B.D. (2002): Teaching the /r/-/l/ discrimination to Japanese adults: behavioural and neural aspects. In: *Physiology & Behavior,* 77, pp. 657-662.

Mitchell, C.J./De Houwer, J./Lovibond, P.F. (2009): The propositional nature of human associative learning. In: *Behavioral and Brain Sciences,* 32, pp. 183–246.

Newell, B.R./Dunn, J.C./Kalish, M. (2011): Systems of category learning: Fact or fantasy? In: *Psychology of Learning and Motivation,* 54, pp. 167-215.

Pearce, J.M. (2008): *Animal learning and cognition.* Hove, UK: Psychology Press.
Shanks, D.R. (1995): *The psychology of associative learning.* Cambridge, UK: Cambridge University Press.
Smith, E.E./Grossman, M. (2008): Multiple systems of category learning. In: *Neuroscience and Biobehavioural Reviews*, 32, pp. 249-264.
Waldron, E.M./Ashby, F.G. (2001): The effects of concurrent task interference on category learning: Evidence for multiple category learning systems. In: *Psychonomic Bulletin and Review,* 8, pp. 168-176.
Weimer, H. (1925): *Psychologie der Fehler.* Leipzig: Klinkhardt.
Wills, A.J. (2005): *New directions in human associative learning.* Lawrence Erlbaum Associates.
Wills, A.J. (2009): Prediction errors and attention in the presence and absence of feedback. In: *Current Directions in Psychological Science,* 18, pp. 95-100.
Wills, A.J./Lavric, A./Croft, G./Hodgson, T.L. (2007): Predictive learning, prediction errors and attention: Evidence from event-related potentials and eye-tracking. In: *Journal of Cognitive Neuroscience.* 19, pp. 843-854.
Zhao, B./Olivera, F. (2006): Error reporting in organizations. In: *Academy of Management Review,* 31, pp. 1012-1030.

Notes

Our new series
Study Guides in Adult Education

ESTHER OLIVER
Research and Development in Adult Education
Fields and Trends
Study Guides in Adult Education
2010. 135 pp. Pb. 16,90 € (D), 17,40 € (A), 25,90 SFr, US$ 25.95, GBP 15,95
ISBN 978-3-86649-304-9

The importance of adult education has been growing steadily, whether it's with regard to migration, societal inclusion, the work place, or the professionalization of adult educators themselves. By providing an international perspective on the most important research issues in adult education, this study guide offers a wealth of up-to-date information for anyone interested in this diverse field. The book is designed as a text book providing didactic material for discussion and further exploration of a wide range of adult education research from an international perspective.

Verlag Barbara Budrich • Barbara Budrich Publishers
Stauffenbergstr. 7. D-51379 Leverkusen Opladen
Tel +49 (0)2171.344.594 • Fax +49 (0)2171.344.693 • info@budrich-verlag.de
US-office: Uschi Golden • 28347 Ridgebrook • Farmington Hills, MI 48334 • USA •
ph +1.248.488.9153 • info@barbara-budrich.net • www.barbara-budrich.net

www.barbara-budrich.net

International issues

MEINERT A. MEYER & BRIAN HUDSON (EDS.)
Beyond Fragmentation: Didactics, Learning and Teaching

2011. Ca. 350 pp. Pb.
Ca. 36,00 € (D), US$ 52.00, GBP 32,95
ISBN 978-3-86649-387-2

It is well known that didactics is not a university discipline in its own right in the English-speaking countries. However, it is firmly rooted in France, Germany, the Nordic countries, Russia, and many other countries in continental Europe. Obviously, national and local differences in the practice of learning and teaching coincide with differences in concept-building.

NICOLE HOLLENBACH & KLAUS-JÜRGEN TILLMANN (EDS.)
Teacher Research and School Development

German approaches and international perspectives
Published in cooperation with Julius Klinkhardt Verlag
2011. 256 pp. Pb. 29,90 € (D), US$45.95, GBP 26,95
ISBN 978-3-86649-352-0

Action research is a specific approach to empirical school research. In fourteen articles different authors explain, how, why and under which circumstances AR – done by teachers and focused on practice-related problems in schools – can initiate curriculum development and help teachers to increase their professionalism.

Verlag Barbara Budrich • Barbara Budrich Publishers
Stauffenbergstr. 7. D-51379 Leverkusen Opladen
Tel +49 (0)2171.344.594 • Fax +49 (0)2171.344.693 • info@budrich-verlag.de
US-office: Uschi Golden • 28347 Ridgebrook • Farmington Hills, MI 48334 • USA •
ph +1.248.488.9153 • info@barbara-budrich.com • www.barbara-budrich.net

www.barbara-budrich.net